PRAISE FOR
YOU (DON'T) SUCK

"What Max has created in this work is a gentle journey into introspection of imposter syndrome. They have skillfully woven information, personal narrative, and exercises to walk with the reader and invite them to learn about and explore the influence of imposter syndrome in 4 key life domains. The way this is done helps the reader to see and understand themselves in affirming ways, and with an opportunity to use the exercises to support their overall growth and well-being."

– Megan Murk (she/her), National Board Certified Coach (NBC-HWC)

"Imposter syndrome used to hold me back from my potential and I wish I had this book years ago. Using easy-to-follow exercises and prompts, this book provides a roadmap that can help you move from burnout to self-empowerment. I particularly like how Max uses their own stories and journey to model this transformation."

– Bernadette Smith (she/her),
CEO Equality Institute and bestselling author of "Inclusive 360"

"Imposter syndrome has impacted me and my life in so many ways. I wish I'd had a book early in my career that could move me beyond these beliefs I picked up from years of people telling me I wasn't good enough. The book is finally here! Max's practical, thoughtful guide will help you regain your power and step into your best self."

– Melinda Briana Epler (she/her),
Founder & CEO, Change Catalyst, and author of "How to Be an Ally"

"In this raw and real exploration of imposter syndrome, Max Masure encourages the reader to ask themselves who benefits when they abandon their inner power. By helping you understand the relationship between your inner landscape and external systems, Masure gives you an actionable and motivating guide to turning down the volume on your imposter syndrome so you can trust yourself and your communities of support more. The result: A stronger sense of self and a more empowered life."

– Kat Vellos (she/her), Author of "We Should Get Together:
The Secret to Cultivating Better Friendships" weshouldgettogether.com

"I recently learned of a concept in early childhood development called healing narrative, an innate way for our young minds to make sense of the world through stories. Stories have dominated my life and not all of them have been healthy. In this book, Max dives deep into the stories we tell ourselves, the stories that hold us back, and the new stories that are within us that need to be read out loud."

– George Aye (he/him), Co-Founder Greater Good Studio

"There is no better time than this very instance to take on what Max is asking for us to do, which is to reframe our self-worth and re-center what most animates us in life, as the true guiding posts and metrics of success. I'm humbled by these self-reflecting questions and raw personal stories. As an equity designer myself, I too am often swept away by the incessant narratives of capitalism and racism to aim for money and quantity as impact, rather than ensuring that the people who are most harmed by these systems are better-off. This book offers a critical anchor for anyone committed to designing a just world, and Max reminds us that it MUST begin with interrogating ourselves."

– Boyuan Gao (she/her), Principal & Partner at Project Inkblot

"A very helpful practical guide for self-reflection! The openness with which Max shares their own journey from self-doubts and struggles towards self-acceptance and pride are an inspiration for everyone! Take a step aside and look at life with acceptance and warmth - and thus make it richer and more fulfilling!"

– Birgit Mager (she/her), President Service Design Network

"Lots of great ways to approach imposter syndrome in my everyday life, good easy activities. Inspiring, vulnerable, enlightening."

"A very insightful and gentle guide to your most inner depths to uncover and eventually eliminate what is holding you down."

"We talk about the human elements and lived experiences within the design industry, but I think we sometimes forget to think about our own experience as professionals. Imposter syndrome is one of those very common experiences in which we may feel like we are alone when in fact, there are so many others who feel the same. Max's work normalizes dialogue around this topic, which is the essential first step. It is tremendously useful on a practical level but it also reminds us that coming together to strengthen our own experiences also builds resilience within our individual communities and the design community at large."

"The path to finding your own measure of success is more complicated than ever—no wonder we doubt and undermine ourselves. Max is the perfect person to help us get the perspective we need to find meaning and joy in our work!"

"Max Masure has created a book that combines personal storytelling and self-reflective activities all with the goal of seeing you through your own imposter syndrome and connecting with your true and authentic self. Using a memoir-like approach, Max shares their successes and challenges on the path to being true to who they are with a deeply moving and vulnerable approach. I'm hard-pressed to think of anyone who wouldn't be able to connect to the raw honesty and courage Max has modeled inspiring us to be free of our own constraints and to live a life that mirrors who we truly are."

YOU DON'T SUCK

HOW TO OVERCOME IMPOSTER SYNDROME

MAX MASURE
they/them

For permission requests, write to the below address:

PYP Academy Press
141 Weston Street, #155
Hartford, CT 06141

The opinions expressed by the Author are not necessarily those held by PYP Academy Press.

Ordering Information: Quantity sales and special discounts are available on quantity purchases by corporations, associations, and others. For details, contact the author at max@youdontsuck-book.com or YouDontSuck-book.com.

Book doula: Rowan Reyes (they/them)
Edited by: August Li (he/him)
Cover design by: Nelly Murariu (she/her)
Typeset by: Max Masure (they/them) with the fonts Adobe Garamond Pro and Acumin Variable Concept

Printed in the United States of America.
ISBN: 978-1-955985-43-7 (paperback)
ISBN: 978-1-955985-44-4 (ebook)

Library of Congress Control Number: 2022900821

First edition, March, 2022.

Publish Your Purpose is a hybrid publisher of non-fiction books. Our authors are thought leaders, experts in their fields, and visionaries paving the way to social change—from food security to anti-racism. We give underrepresented voices power and a stage to share their stories, speak their truth, and impact their communities. Do you have a book idea you would like us to consider publishing? Please visit PublishYourPurpose.com for more information.

This book is dedicated to Sophie: you didn't suck.

CONTENTS

OVERCOMING IMPOSTER SYNDROME WORKSHOPS

Take your learning to the next level by joining an online workshop with Max Masure and like-minded folks interested in overcoming imposter syndrome.

"This workshop provides a supportive space to honestly reflect on your work without shame. Grounding, open, honest."
– workshop participant

"Such a welcoming and caring community, that feels safe, was integral for learning. Vulnerable, intimate, welcoming."
– workshop participant

"I'd recommend it to everyone! (...) Let gentle Max guide you in a space of non-judgment - truly a wonderful guide. Enlightening, beautiful, uniting."
– workshop participant

"Typically I'm very uncomfortable with workshops and sharing, especially when it's related to vulnerability. This was empowering and I was very comfortable throughout. I felt like I could be honest with myself and sharing was optional. Very refreshing."
– workshop participant

YOUDONTSUCK-BOOK.COM

FOREWORD

You are good at what you do.

You will hopefully be better at what you do tomorrow than you were yesterday. But that doesn't mean that you aren't good at it today. Wanting to be better at something is healthy. Not appreciating how good you already are is unhealthy.

You are good at what you do.

Write it on a post-it. Tape it to your laptop. Make some of that motivational art that's all over Instagram. Tattoo it on yourself. Write it on a cake. Just believe it.

Acknowledging that you are good at what you do is a gift that you give to the people you interact with. You are a professional with a skillset. Throughout your life you will interact with other professionals who have skillsets that you need. When you sit in a stylist's hair you want the stylist to believe they're good at what they do. When you walk into an unfamiliar restaurant and ask the server to recommend something from the menu you want them to believe they're good at what they do. If we call a plumber to fix a leaky faucet we want the plumber to believe they are good at what they do. And if you're unfortunate enough to run into an emergency room with your thumb in a ziploc bag after a bagel cutting accident you want the medical staff to believe they are good at what they do.

Our confidence is a gift that puts the people who interact with us at ease. It tells them they're in good hands. It puts them at ease. And it reassures them they're in the right place talking to the right person.

Throughout this book, Max is going to take you on an amazing journey to rid you of your self-doubt. Max can do this because they are good at what they do. So are you.

Our confidence is a gift that tells people they will be ok.

Our confidence tells other people they can accept our help. And, lordy, everyone can use a little extra help right now.

Mike Monteiro

INTRODUCTION

Picking up this book is your first step to trusting yourself and growing your inner power.

I wrote this book for the person I was five years ago when I was lost and burning out, completely misaligned with my inner self. I wish I had this guide to support me.

In this workbook, you will find transformative activities that I designed and experimented with hundreds of workshop attendees over the past three years.

My hope is that you learn from my own journey so you can avoid some of the rough paths I had to take. Consider me and this book as your supportive cheerleaders to your growth into believing these words: you don't suck. On the contrary, you rock and you are doing amazing.

Max Masure

THE BURNOUT
THAT SAVED MY LIFE

I burned out at thirty-five.

At that time, I pretty much checked all the boxes: a successful woman working as an international designer, married, a kid, a big apartment in Brooklyn, NY. I forgot one thing in my plan: myself.

I spent a week at the hospital with a high fever, and I had to stop working for three months. My brain did not work anymore. It froze every time I opened my laptop and tried to focus on a task. It was frightening as I used to spend twelve hours a day on my computer, even on weekends. Now I wondered:

What will I do for a living if I can't work like this?

I worked as a tech designer. I consulted for clients who launched tech products and services into the world. Their goal included getting millions of users and making investors happy. As a designer I should have aimed to advocate for ethics and made sure the people who used their products would not be harmed or put in danger. When we design in a silo without consulting the potential users, we risk building a product only for the elite with money, time, and resources.

For example, Airbnb seemed like a genius idea: renting your place for travelers. But they didn't think about the ethics. We now have a situation where low-income city inhabitants cannot find affordable housing because many landlords have turned their properties into permanent Airbnb places.

Simply said, many tech companies do not care about the impact of their products on underrepresented folks. And by helping them, I contributed to the problem.

At the time, I had severe imposter syndrome and acted as a people pleaser, saying yes to everything a person, a client, or an employer asked from me.

I was terrified of disappointing someone. I would rather compromise my values than face a disagreement. I would agree to design ethically problematic features, believing we should focus on making more money rather than releasing a fair and community-centered product.

Burning out was the tip of the iceberg that would reveal powerful parts of myself.

When It Happened

My burnout happened just before Trump got elected President of the US in 2016. That day woke me up. What this government would do to remove rights from underrepresented folks would lead to a disaster. I even looked into moving to another country but decided I could make an impact locally. But how?

Through my burnout recovery, I started to see a path to become a social justice designer, a community-centered designer advocating for underrepresented folks. The more space I found in my brain by resting and doing therapy, the less my identity as a cisgender, heterosexual woman felt like myself. In January 2017, I started to see a glimpse of who I would become: Max.

It took just a few more months to come out fully to myself as a transmasculine person. By May that same year, I started hormone therapy and grew into a free version of myself. It surprised me as much as the people around me. I began to understand the value of boundaries and being clear on what I could give.

Three years after burning out, I finally felt grounded and assertive about my boundaries without fear. I relied on my community without shame, and I envisioned a positive future without scarcity. I wish I'd had more keys when I fought my imposter syndrome, and this is why I put this book together with what helped me overcome it. I should say "tame my imposter syndrome;" it never really goes away, but we can learn how to respond to it.

How Many Tasks

The first therapist I saw after my burnout asked me: "How many tasks do you have on your to-do list every day?"

With the cadence I imposed on myself, I had twenty daily tasks, only counting my work. It did not seem a lot for me as I used to proudly identify myself as efficient and fast, qualities I considered inherent to being a good UX/UI designer.

His following question shocked me. It even felt silly. "How many tasks do you accomplish out of those twenty?"

I bluntly replied, "Well, twenty-one. Why? People do it differently?"

It did not occur to me that I didn't have to accomplish all the tasks on a daily to-do list. Disappointing others brought terror in me; the feeling of accomplishment generated all of my adrenaline and pleasure. I realized that when I couldn't list my top five priorities. I could only think of work and my current projects. As we will see later in this book, I now know these are symptoms of the Solo and the Expert Imposter Syndromes.

My therapist challenged me to only put eight items on my daily list, including personal stuff like picking up my kid at daycare or having a coffee with a friend. Eight! Instead of twenty. It took me a few months to achieve this, and it completely transformed me.

Those three months I had to take off to mentally recover and build a better work-life balance taught me to focus on my own needs and priorities. That space allowed me to think about myself and my desires instead of trying to please everyone.

Do you feel like you wish you had more time to relax, do nothing?
Taking the time to slow down and remember what we like doing is the first step to listening to ourselves.
This activity will help us discover our inner needs.

I wish I had time to

☐ _____

☐ _____

☐ _____

☐ _____

☐ _____

☐ _____

☐ _____

☐ _____

Instead, I'm giving my time to

☐ _____

☐ _____

☐ _____

☐ _____

☐ _____

☐ _____

☐ _____

☐ _____

I don't make time for it because

Doing nothing makes me feel

_____

_____

_____

_____

_____

_____

_____

Like me, let's try to plan our day with four tasks we need to do, two that would be nice if we do them, and two last ones that we know there is no way we can do today. Make sure to add one activity you wish you had time to do from the previous exercise!

Need to do

☐ _____

☐ _____

☐ _____

☐ _____

Would be nice

☐ _____

☐ _____

No way I can do this today

☐ _____

☐ _____

WE DON'T SUCK!

In the following chapters, I'll help us believe in that sentence. I know this is sometimes impossible to imagine, and this is why we are in this together.

I want this book to support us in demystifying imposter syndrome and discovering ourselves so we can thrive without going through the burnout I went through. I want to use my bumpy journey to help us reach our inner power. And I've got a plan!

First, I am offering an assessment to take a deep look into how we situate ourselves in the imposter syndrome spectrum. I crafted an easy and quick questionnaire that will help us draw our own Imposter Syndrome Radar.

Then, I'll share more about my journey as we go through listening to our needs, setting our boundaries, reimagining who we are, accessing our inner power, and finding our interdependent community.

In every chapter, I am offering interactive activities. We will build our vetting grid to decide who we should work with (or not!), rephrase our fear and anxiety, imagine the worst and prevent it from happening, and build our Success Tree to remind ourselves that we know what we are doing. I'll guide us into believing that luck has nothing to do with it.

But first of all, what is imposter syndrome, and who has it?

WE
DON'T
SUCK

WHAT IS IMPOSTER SYNDROME, AND WHO HAS IT?

While this book primarily focuses on demystifying and overcoming imposter syndrome, it also discusses why we have imposter syndrome. Let's start by understanding the different types of imposter syndrome. We might relate to one or more archetypes of imposter syndrome (source: www. verywellhealth.com): the perfectionist, the expert, the soloist, the natural genius, the superhero.

PERFECTIONIST

We focus on how we did something, and we feel like a failure with even the slightest mistake.

I recognize myself when I

_____

_____

_____

_____

_____

_____

EXPERT

We are concerned about what or how much we know or can do. We feel like a failure if we have even a slight lack of knowledge in something.

I recognize myself when I

SOLOIST

We care about the "who." We feel we cannot take help from others if we want to be successful.

I recognize myself when I

_____

_____

_____

_____

_____

NATURAL GENIUS

We measure our worth by how and when accomplishments happen in terms of ease and speed. We are ashamed to take extra time or need to redo something.

I recognize myself when I

_____

_____

_____

_____

_____

SUPERHERO

We measure our accomplishments by how many roles we can juggle and excel in.

I recognize myself when I

_____

_____

_____

_____

_____

In all honesty, I still struggle with these behaviors myself. I have the superhero imposter syndrome, always jumping into a new project, even though I keep complaining that I do too much. Writing this book tapped into my natural genius imposter syndrome: it was hard to rework the manuscript so many times. I expected the first draft to be perfect, and my editor's feedback hit my ego. But I kept going because I owned the tools to cope and change my thinking habits. And I am excited to share them all in this book!

The Workbook to Overcome Imposter Syndrome

I revisited the subtitle of the book, "The workbook to debunk imposter syndrome," after I received feedback from psychologists that debunking meant proving that something is untrue, meaning impostor syndrome did not exist.

Imposter syndrome is real and linked with our external and internal relationships with power. I understand it as the internal dialogue to protect us from danger — but we grow when taking risks. So imposter syndrome can be helpful if we don't let it control us.

How can we know if we have imposter syndrome?:

- We are incapable of acknowledging our success.

- We are incapable of celebrating success, too worried about what we have to do next.

- If we are successful, we assume it's because of someone else, or we were lucky and not that our success results from hard work.

- We always focus on the minor parts that were not that good, completely dismissing the significant elements that were successful.

- We feel like we are not doing enough, and someone will soon discover that we are frauds.

When I started writing this book, I wanted to learn more about imposter syndrome. I created a questionnaire with four categories to understand how common imposter syndrome is and how it affects underrepresented folks.

I recruited one hundred people with different identities. Seventy-two percent of them were cisgender (meaning their gender aligns with their gender assigned at birth). Twenty-eight percent were transgender or gender-nonconforming (meaning their gender differs from the gender assigned at birth).

Thirty percent of the participants were Black, Indigenous, or a Person of Color, while seventy percent were white.

The participants indicated whether they agreed or disagreed with each statement.

1. Listening to Our Needs and Setting Our Boundaries

This section is about how we interact with others, what we let others do to us, and when we speak up to protect our wellbeing.

Statements were:

- I feel pressure to work at a rushed pace

- I make it a requirement for myself to accomplish all my tasks on my daily work to-do list

- I reply to work emails after work or on weekends

- I feel pressured to work during my weekend if my manager asks me to get something ready by Monday

- I go along with a decision an authority made, despite feeling ethical conflict

- I feel at risk of losing my job if I speak up about some issues

2. Reimagining Who We Want to Be

This section addresses how we see ourselves in the future, how we feel about our goals in life, and how we are aligned with them now.

Statements were:

- I go along with a decision even though I disagree with it

- I regularly imagine the worst-case scenario using "What if…" sentences

- I am nervous when I think about next year

- I don't feel confident that I can reach my goals

- I feel very uncomfortable when someone asks me about my goals

- I have a hard time not thinking about the potential failure of my ideas and projects

3. Accessing Our Inner Power

This section examines how we trust ourselves over external pressure and how close we are to being our true selves.

Statements were:

- I feel like I don't do enough to prove that my work is good

- I work after hours or on weekends to make sure my work will be perfect

- I get nervous waiting for feedback from a manager

- I hesitate to express an opinion when interacting with people in power

- I see some unethical patterns/decisions, but I do not speak up

- I sometimes feel confused about my perspective due to the opinions of others

4. Finding Our Interdependent Community

This section is about how we rely on others to be successful, our relationship with shame, and how we plan for future situations.

Statements were:

- I usually isolate myself when I feel disappointed

- I feel incapable of talking to someone when I feel stuck or discouraged

- I feel like I have to solve every problem by myself

- I feel uncomfortable talking about my challenges with others

- I feel like everyone has their life together except me

- I rarely know which person or community I can reach out to

I ran the study for a month and collected one hundred answers. It is not scientific research, but more like testing the water and understanding how I could support my peers in the best way possible.

I had no clue what the conclusions would be. It was eye-opening to discover the overwhelming results. Sixty percent of the people who answered the questionnaire felt like they didn't do enough to prove that their work was good.

WE ARE ~~DOING~~ ENOUGH

Do We All Have Imposter Syndrome?

When I started creating this workbook about imposter syndrome, I knew I wanted to offer activities and exercises to empower people. I initially wanted to support folks who had burnout or were close to crashing down, but I realized through the survey that it touches more people than I thought, across different levels of position at work, race, and gender.

Studies show that underrepresented people like women are assumed to be less competent than men (Pew Research Center, 2017). People of Color are less likely to have a job interview (Whitened Resumes: Race and Self-Presentation in the Labor Market). The fact that marginalized folks need to change jobs more often by feeling like they don't belong in a workplace brings some self-doubt. These facts increase the chances of having imposter syndrome. Rebekah Bastian elaborates on this topic in her article "Why Imposter Syndrome Hits Underrepresented Identities Harder, And How Employers Can Help."

I wanted to see if my survey would show similar differences. To the question "I feel like I don't do enough to prove that my work is good," I received a similar sixty percent across gender and race, with even a slightly higher score for Yes for the white people who answered my survey.

Feeling disempowered by not expressing our opinion by fear of retaliation can result in low self-esteem and losing confidence. It didn't surprise me that Black, Indigenous, and People of Color and trans and gender-nonconforming people have a higher rate of feeling disempowered and struggling when talking with someone in power.

I feel like I don't do enough to prove that my work is good

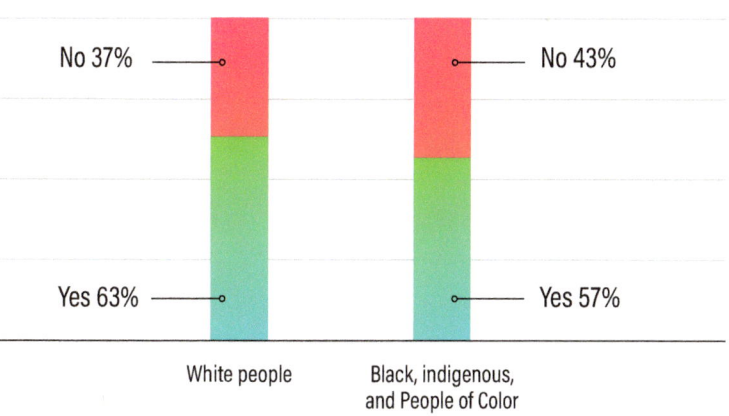

No 37% —— White people

No 43% —— Black, indigenous, and People of Color

Yes 63%

Yes 57%

I feel like I don't do enough to prove that my work is good

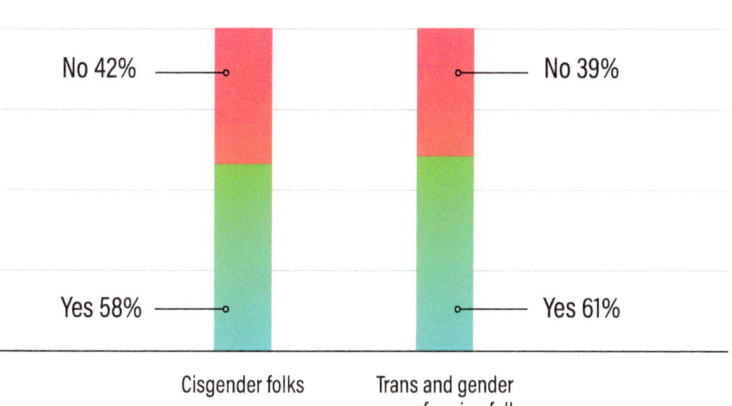

No 42% —— Cisgender folks

No 39% —— Trans and gender nonconforming folks

Yes 58%

Yes 61%

It surprised me to discover that cisgender white men also have trouble expressing their opinions when interacting with people in power. I anticipated to see a massive difference on this chart with cisgender women and trans and gender-nonconforming people having more trouble than cisgender white men.

I hesitate to express an opinion when interacting with people in power

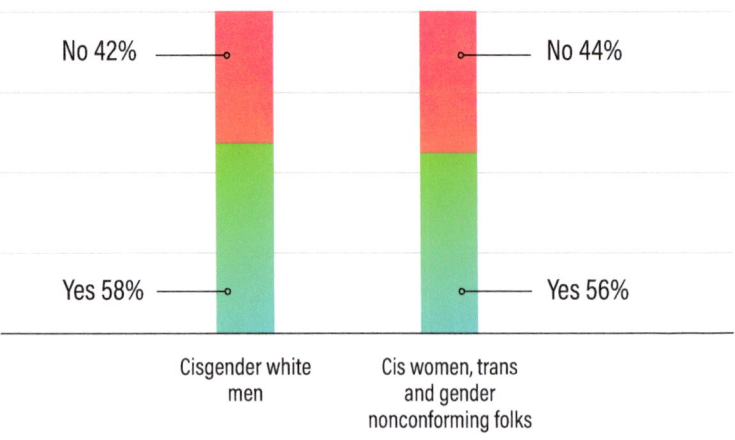

No 42% ——— No 44%

Yes 58% ——— Yes 56%

Cisgender white men

Cis women, trans and gender nonconforming folks

I planned to have a chapter about how underrepresented folks have more chances to have imposter syndrome due to oppressive systems and the lack of encouragement and trust from the get-go. But my conclusion from this isolated and small research with one hundred people is that imposter syndrome also touches cisgender men and women and white people. We are all victims of the way the designed systems do not value us.

Sixty-five percent answered, "I have a hard time not thinking about the potential failure of my ideas and projects."

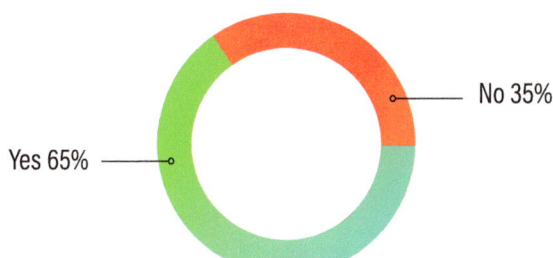

No 35%

Yes 65%

Sixty-seven percent agreed with the statement, "I go along with a decision even though I disagreed with it."

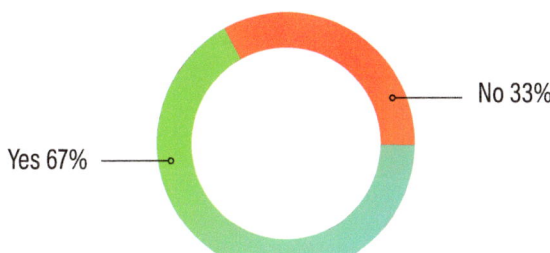

No 33%

Yes 67%

Sixty-six percent said, "I am nervous when I think about next year."

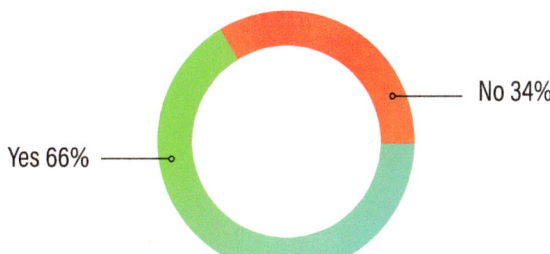

No 34%

Yes 66%

Who Do We See As An Authority?

I learned through my burnout experience that external and internal pressure make us forget about our power. We are dependent on others' approval, usually from an authority (our manager, our boss, our client, a mentor), and we slowly lose the capacity to do tasks as simple as writing an email without self-doubt. It creates a vicious cycle that reinforces the sense that we are not capable.

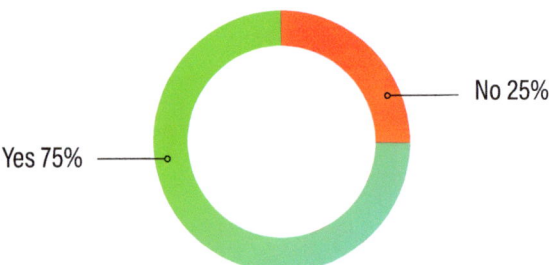

Seventy-five percent said,
"I get nervous waiting for feedback from a manager."

No 25%

Yes 75%

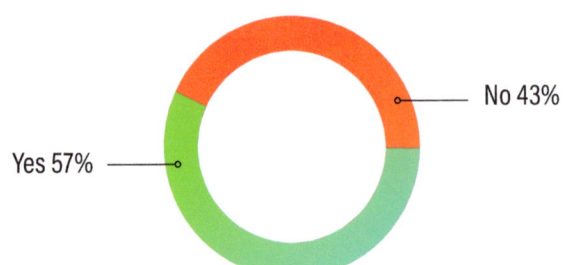

Fifty-seven percent said,
"I hesitate to express an opinion when interacting with people in power."

No 43%

Yes 57%

Sixty-two percent said, "I sometimes feel confused about my perspective due to the views of others."

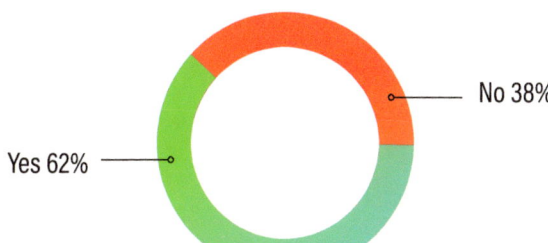

No 38%

Yes 62%

Seventy-seven percent said, "I feel pressure to work at a rushed pace."

No 23%

Yes 77%

Sixty percent said, "I reply to work emails after work or on weekends."

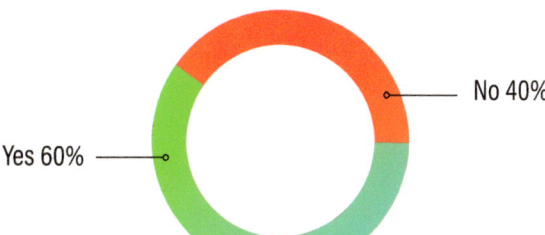

No 40%

Yes 60%

W
BENE
FROM
SELF-D

HO
FITS
MY
OUBT?

Who Benefit From My Self-Doubt?

As you can see, we are not alone with these feelings! And this is a part to hold onto: we tend to isolate ourselves when we doubt ourselves as if we cannot show up to the world if we are not our best selves. It might seem contradictory, but the opposite is what can free us from the power of our imposter syndrome. Surrounding ourselves with genuine folks with whom we can be vulnerable and finding support is vital to liberate ourselves from the anxiety and the low self-esteem when imposter syndrome overcomes us.

Seventy-five percent said,
"I usually isolate myself when I feel disappointed."

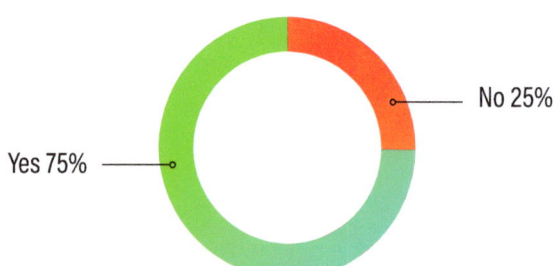

Fifty-six percent said, "I feel like I have to solve every problem by myself."

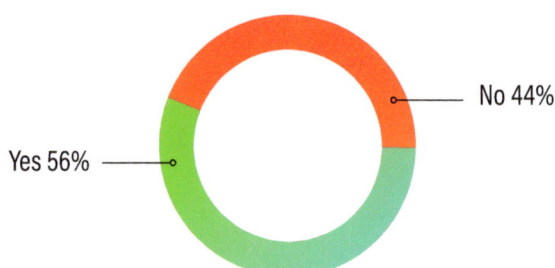

I ask myself, "Who is benefiting from my self-doubts? Who wants to see me abandon my power?" In the society we live in, power is the currency. The well-designed system in place actively tries to disempower us to protect the ones in position of power. The less we believe in ourselves, the easier it is to abuse us and remove our strength.

We all benefit from speaking up and being assertive. Our inner power depends on it.

How to Overcome Imposter Syndrome

There is no unique way to trust and grow our confidence, but here are the four areas we will work on:

- Listening to Our Needs and Setting Our Boundaries

- Reimagining Who We Want to Be

- Accessing Our Inner Power

- Finding Our Interdependent Community

These four areas are the four main chapters of this book and the four parts of the imposter syndrome survey I launched and that you will take yourself soon. It translates into a radar chart to see the topics we need to pay attention to and improve with the tools I crafted for my workshops and this book.

The closer the dot is to the center of the circle, the less power we have. The ideal radar chart would have an extending shape where all our parts are fully empowered.

We will see on the following page my chart at the beginning of my journey.

When I struggled the most with imposter syndrome ten years ago,
I had a constricted shape on my radar.

BOUNDARIES

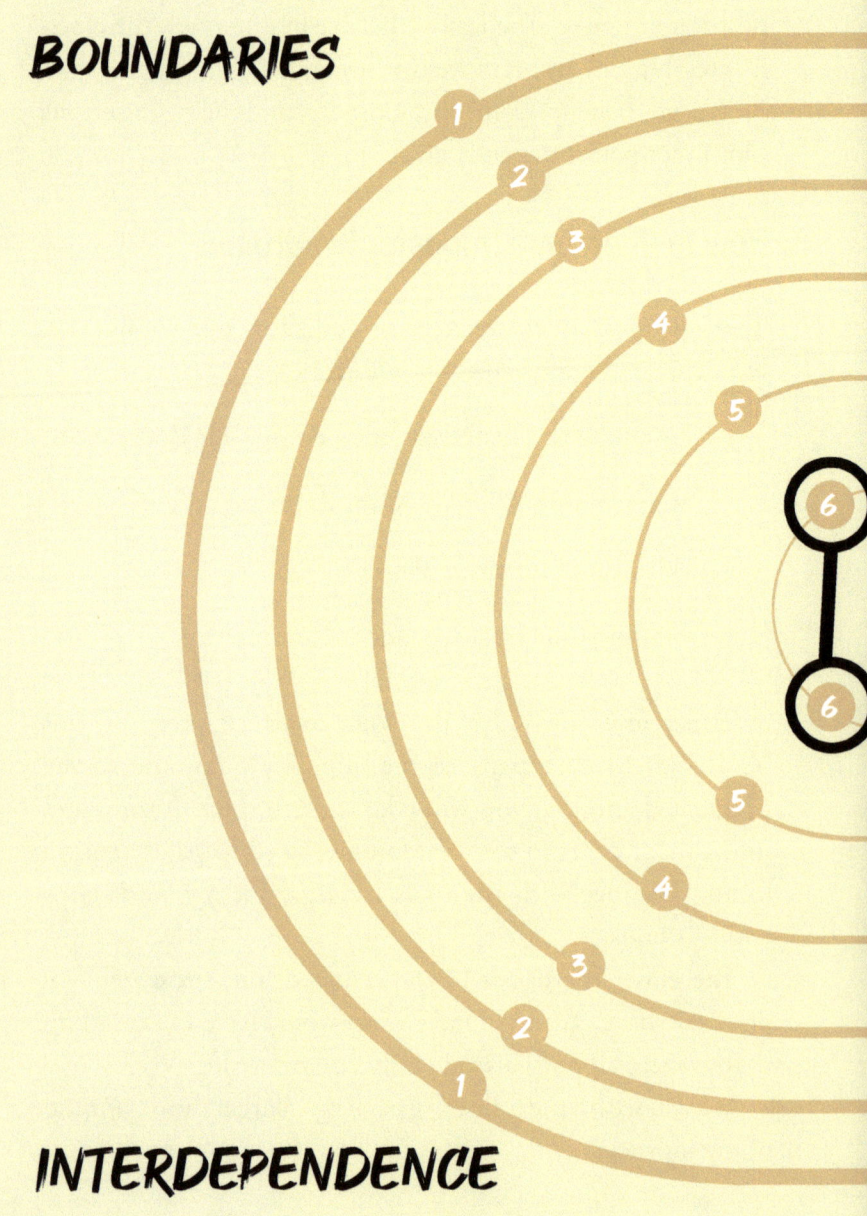

INTERDEPENDENCE

FUTURE SELF

INNER POWER

Flash forward to today: it doesn't seem that I am dominated by imposter syndrome anymore but could still benefit from interdependent community (step 4 in this book).

BOUNDARIES

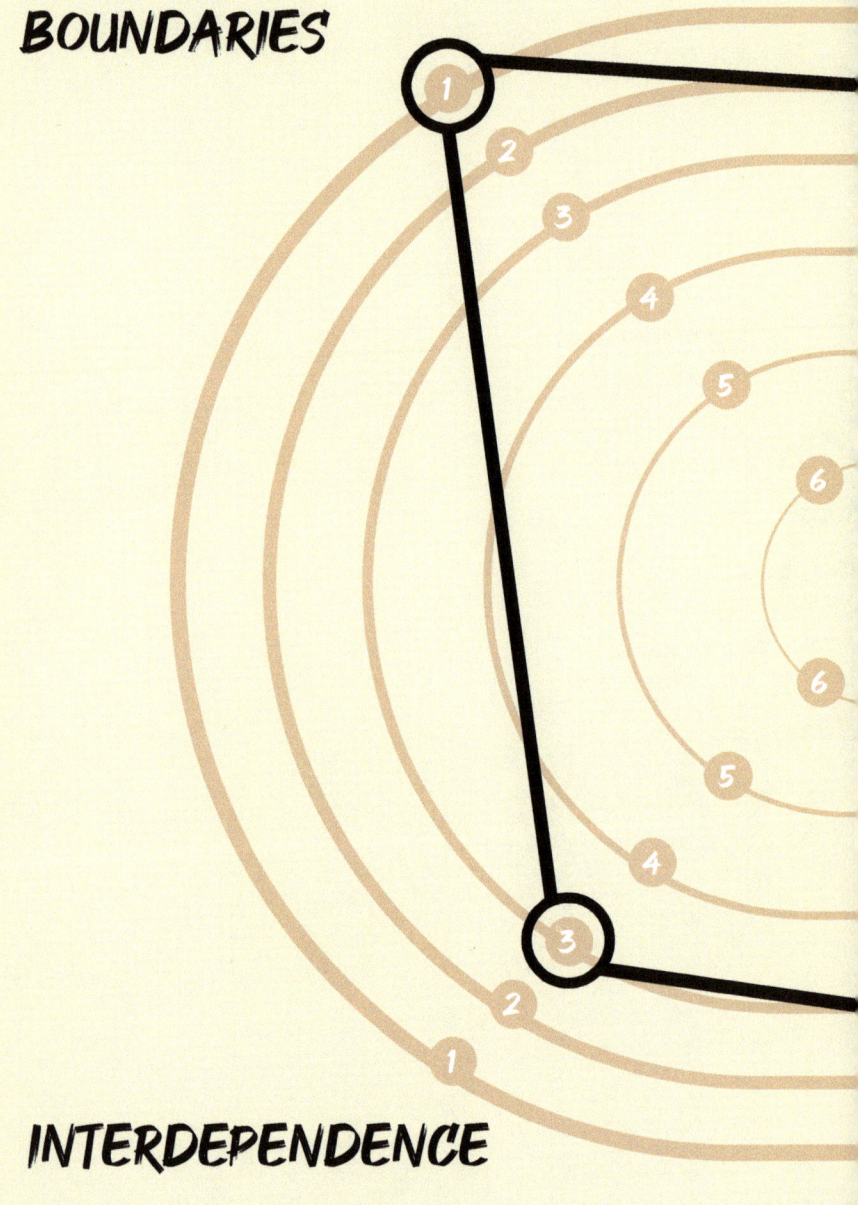

INTERDEPENDENCE

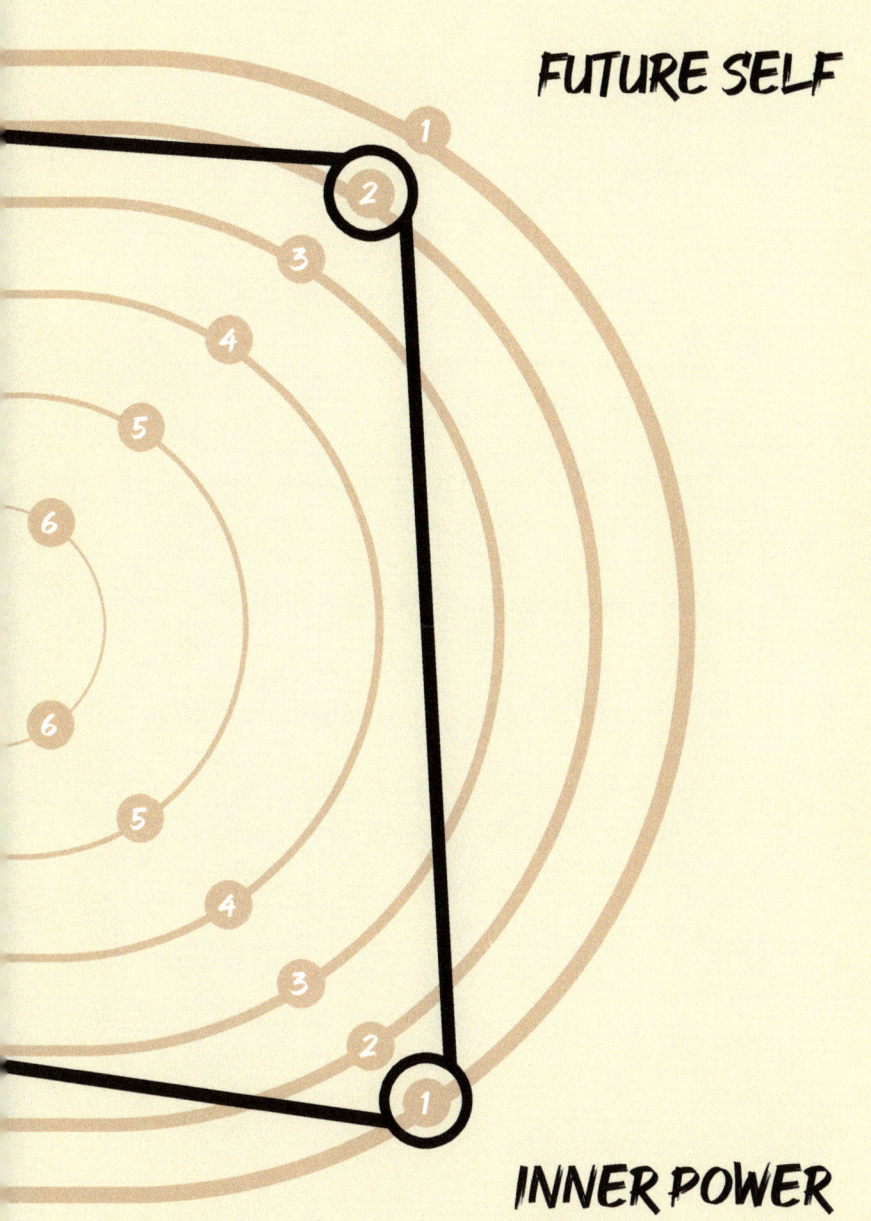

FUTURE SELF

INNER POWER

Now it's your turn to discover the areas where you might have some imposter syndrome. Don't worry. This workbook is here to support you in overcoming it! Read each statement and check the box if you agree with it.

1. Listening to our needs and setting our boundaries

☐ I feel pressure to work at a rushed pace

☐ I make it a requirement for myself to accomplish all my tasks on my daily work to-do list

☐ I go along with a decision an authority made, despite feeling ethical conflict

☐ I feel at risk of losing my job if I speak up about some issues

☐ I reply to work emails after work or on weekends

☐ I feel pressured to work during my weekend if my manager asks me to get something ready by Monday

___ / 6

I got three or more

It seems like you might want to work on your needs and boundaries. I know it can feel intimidating, but the first step of this book is here to support you! You will find tools to feel more in control.

I got two or less

You seem to have identified your needs and are pretty good with your boundaries. Great job! You might find additional tools in the first step of this book.

This result makes me feel

_____

_____

2. Reimagining who we want to be

- [ ] I go along with a decision even though I disagreed with it
- [ ] I regularly imagine the worst-case scenario using "What if…" sentences
- [ ] I am nervous when I think about next year
- [ ] I don't feel confident that I can reach my goals
- [ ] I feel very uncomfortable when someone asks me about my goals
- [ ] I have a hard time not thinking about the potential failure of my ideas and projects

___ / 6

I got three or more

It seems like you have some difficulties to imagine yourself in the future, to visualize your future self. But with a bit of imagination we can do it, as you will see in the second step of this book.

I got two or less

Good job believing in yourself! When we can see our goal, it's easier to reach it. You might be able to take it a bit further with the help of the second step of this book.

This result makes me feel

_____

_____

3. Accessing our inner power

☐ I feel like I don't do enough to prove that my work is good

☐ I work after hours or on weekends to make sure my work will be perfect

☐ I get nervous waiting for feedback from a manager

☐ I hesitate to express an opinion when interacting with people in power

☐ I see some unethical patterns/decisions, but I do not speak up

☐ I sometimes feel confused about my perspective due to the opinions of others

___ / 6

I got three or more

I feel you. It is hard to stand up for ourselves. The third step on this book is all about inner power and speaking up. Don't worry, I got you!

I got two or less

Yes! Kudos to you for respecting yourself. You might create even more habits following the third step of this book.

This result makes me feel

_____

_____

4. Finding our interdependent community

- [ ] I usually isolate myself when I feel disappointed
- [ ] I feel incapable of talking to someone when I feel stuck or discouraged
- [ ] I feel like I have to solve every problem by myself
- [ ] I feel uncomfortable talking about my challenges with others
- [ ] I feel like everyone has their life together except me
- [ ] I rarely know which person or community I can reach out to

___ / 6

I got three or more

First of all, you are not alone. Even if that's how it feels some days. The last step of this book will remind you of your community and how we flourish when we are surrounded by our support team.

I got two or less

So great that you already rely on your community! Such a big deal. It does help, right? On the last step of this book you might solidify even more your support system.

This result makes me feel

_____

_____

Report the results from the previous pages: a number six will be put on the smaller circle at the center, while a number one will be on the larger outside circle.

BOUNDARIES

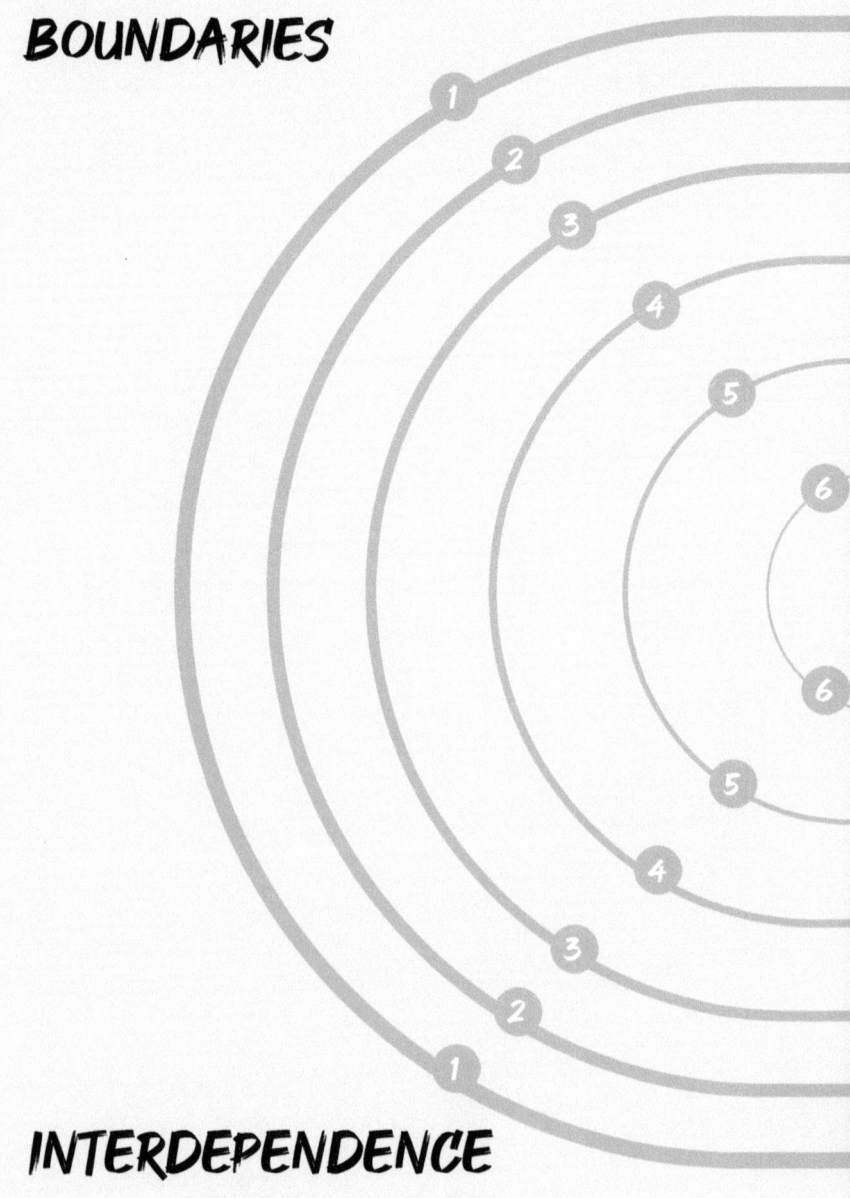

INTERDEPENDENCE

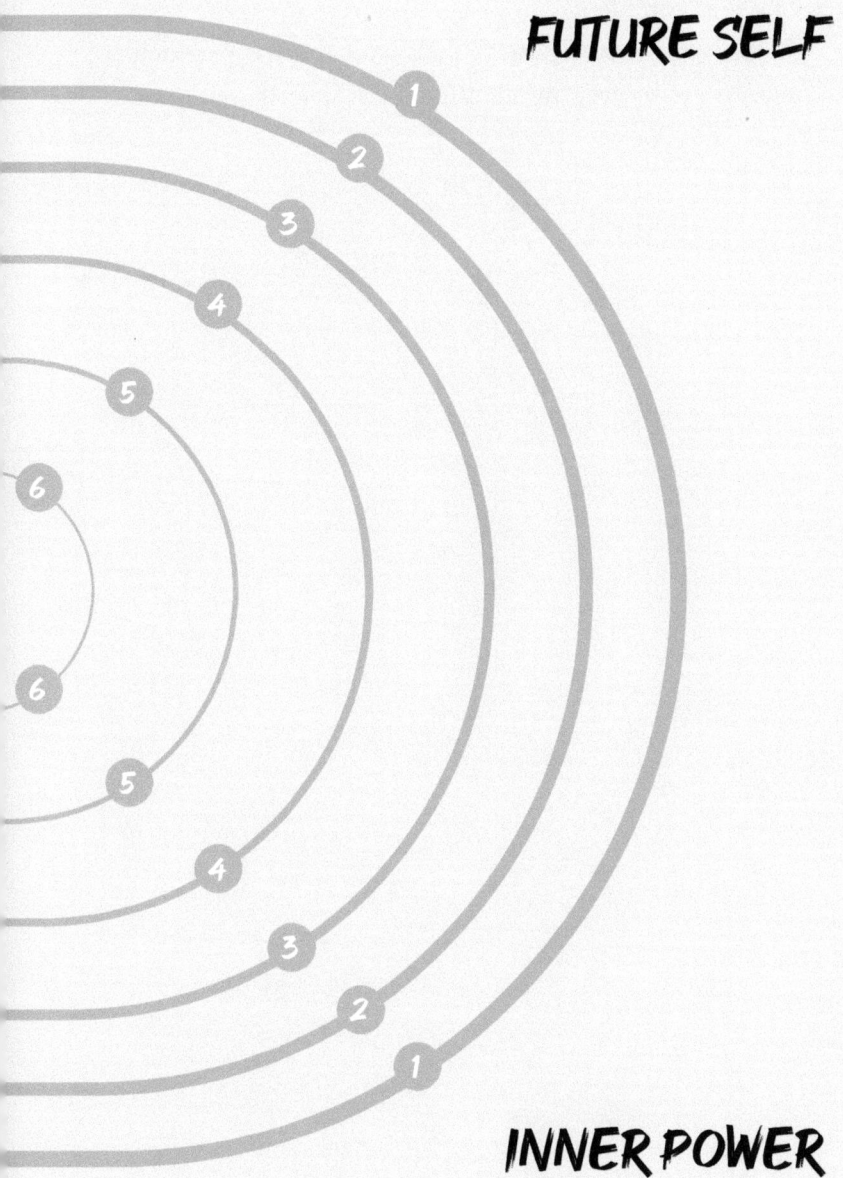

FUTURE SELF

INNER POWER

Now that we have our imposter syndrome radar, we are ready to improve some areas. Knowing ourselves is a crucial step towards facing imposter syndrome and healing. In the following chapters, we will use tools to increase our self-esteem and confidence.

Before we dive in, I want to share a bit about my particular take on the subject: trans identity and imposter syndrome.

TRANS IDENTITY AND IMPOSTER SYNDROME

I lived my life as a woman for thirty-five years. When I came out as a transmasculine person, my whole world and view radically changed. I woke up from being controlled by our oppressive systems.

My purpose in life is to wake people up. Wake them up from the systems we live in. I am talking about white supremacy and capitalism. The systems that make it almost impossible for us to reach our true selves. Gender is a construct invented to keep gender-nonconforming folks silent, in the same way white people created the race logic to be considered the highest on the race spectrum. I recommend the book "Reinventing Race, Reinviting Racism" edited by John J. Betancur and Cedric Herring (Haymarket Books) and "How to Be an Antiracist" by Ibram X Kendi (One World) to learn more about the invention of race.

Before we dig deeper into imposter syndrome tools, I want to take a moment to share my journey in the hope that it will inspire us to listen to our true selves.

Coming Out as Trans Shook my Imposter Syndrome

In March 2017, I reached rock bottom and concluded that I might not continue to live, at least not as a woman. That day became the scariest and most hopeful day of my life. Coming out as a transgender person at thirty-five took me on a giant leap, a life-or-death kind of leap. Like almost every change in life, it came with fear and hope. It concluded with me giving myself a rebirth.

In the queer community, at least, we talk a lot about gaslighting: when someone makes us believe that what we witnessed or felt was not true, even though we are pretty sure we are right until they insist so much that we start doubting what we saw or felt. We rarely talk about our own gaslighting: I became a master in gaslighting myself, losing confidence and being less and less sure of anything. My imposter syndrome was at the highest before I came out as trans. My mind was misaligned with my body, and every decision I made felt inadequate, awkward, insecure.

On top of that, I grew up in France's misogynistic, binary society where masculine-presenting people are praised and encouraged, which builds their confidence. It is widespread for feminine-presenting persons to talk themselves down, as they are used to feeling less valuable. Since age seven, I knew I rejected my body, but I never had the language to express those feelings. I felt a constant clumsiness in my own body; I avoided mirrors.

I remember watching La Cage aux Folles (literally "the cage of crazy women"), a farce by Jean Poiret. It aired as one of the first mainstream movies that featured drag queens.

At the time, and even now, gay feminine people were identified by the slang "Folles" — "crazy." Movies portrayed transgender persons as jokes, not empowered at all. They taught me to bury deep down any feeling of being different or people would mock me.

On top of that, France has a very gendered culture and language. Every word is either masculine or feminine, and we conjugate every adjective according to the word's gender: "the girl is short" — "la fille est petite"; "the boy is short" –"le garçon est petit." There is no escape from the binary in France. Everyone in stores uses madam or sir to greet people. We are on one side of that binary: woman, who learns how to receive unsolicited comments, or man, who feels entitled to invade someone else's space. I've witnessed firsthand how masculinity can be toxic and make a room feel suddenly unsafe.

We teach women not to walk alone at night and wear "appropriate" clothes not to attract looks and comments. We are living in a world where being female-presenting means that we use half of our day focusing on who might be following us, closing our legs tight when we sit on a subway car, smiling at catcallers in case they get aggressive if we ignore them, fixing our shirt in case our cleavage is too revealing when we enter a meeting room.

Living in this constant fear exhausted me and, in my case, challenged me even more because the female presentation attracting those unsolicited, disturbing sexual comments already caused me so much distress. Late at night, I used to walk closer to female-presenting people to feel safe.

The Balance Between Confidence and Arrogance

Even though I now identify as nonbinary and use they/them pronouns, I initially went through a hyper-masculine phase where I spoke a very gendered vocabulary (like "bro," "dude"…) and used he/him pronouns. I think I felt the need to go into the "bro" culture to counterbalance the femininity I had to experience against my will for thirty-five years. However, I played a dangerous role by being part of the "boys club." It feels safe to be at the top of the food chain, but it also hurts women and everyone in our society who is not a cisgender white man. By perpetuating the idea that male-presenting persons are the most influential individuals and putting masculine terms as neutral like "dude" and "hey guys!" even when the group is not only "guys," we continue to feed the binary gender war. The male privilege means higher salaries, more speaking time in meetings, or overall more credibility to the point that we can get away with murder. We won't challenge this enough until we make the neutral a real neutral between women and men.

I've been aware that exploring my gender made me cross the line of toxic masculinity. I had to stop being a jerk and turn my newly earned privilege into positive actions. Once I received this unfair society as a victim; my contribution will now be to dismantle it.

I understand how cisgender men have a hard time believing that this treatment difference exists and affects someone's mental health and growth. I sometimes even forget that it exists, and I lived for thirty-five years as a woman.

By being seen as a white masculine person, I gain some privileges. What I say is ten times more potent than when

I was read as a woman. I bring up the same feminist and inclusive conversations, with the difference being that now people listen to me. I receive way less noise that tries to shut me down, which allows me to believe in my thoughts and feelings. I need less effort to convince others of my ideas and plans because I seem more trustworthy as a masculine-presenting person.

Why do I feel more confident now? I experienced firsthand that men are overall more encouraged. Being supported fuels my self-esteem, allowing me to take more risks — the secret to growing more confident. Being seen, heard, and believed led to an incredible boost to my growth.

But the real reason is that I overcame my imposter syndrome by being my true self. I accessed my inner power by removing layers that didn't reflect my identity. I finally align with who I am — my authentic self. I spent almost all my life pretending to be someone else — a woman before, then a man, and finally being aligned as my true self, Max. A mix of masculinity and femininity.

We have to be the most authentic with ourselves. In this activity, I will guide us to assess our awareness of gender and ourselves, differentiating what comes from external pressure and what is actually us.

My role models of femininity growing up

- [ ] _____
- [ ] _____
- [ ] _____
- [ ] _____
- [ ] _____
- [ ] _____
- [ ] _____
- [ ] _____

My role models of masculinity growing up

- [ ]
- [ ]
- [ ]
- [ ]
- [ ]
- [ ]
- [ ]
- [ ]

What I learned from them

Messages about gender that I received from the media

What remains true now

_____

_____

_____

_____

_____

_____

What I see differently now

_____

_____

_____

_____

_____

_____

_____

Me as a kid

Gender expression

Masculine   Feminine

Notes

Was feeling like a boy, had mostly boy friends

Me as an adult

Gender expression

Masculine   Feminine

Notes

Was following the archetype of what a woman should look like

Me as my authentic self

Gender expression

Masculine   Feminine

Notes

I am aligned with who I am

Me as a kid

Gender expression

Masculine   Feminine

Notes

_____

_____

Me as an adult

Gender expression

Masculine   Feminine

Notes

Me as my authentic self

Gender expression

Masculine   Feminine

Notes

_____

_____

What did you notice? How did it make you feel?

What was surprising?

SSSSH...
LET'S HEAR
WHAT OUR
INNER POWER
HAS TO SAY.

Finding my Purpose in Life

After discovering my inner self, I still had to fight trans issues like legally changing my name to Max. I had to update it both in France and in the US, so I lived for a very long time with my very feminine birth name on my credit card. One day, I paid for an order at a coffee shop using that card. When she finished preparing my tea, the barista shouted out my birth name, which did not match my masculine presentation at all. In this profoundly traumatic experience, I felt a deep sense of gender dysphoria and fear as this put me at risk as everyone in the cafe became aware of my transgender identity. I wanted to crawl inside my skin; everything instantly seemed too hard and not worth the fight. Nobody would ever see me as I see myself. I wanted to disappear. I wanted to die.

I picked up my tea, grumbled that my name was actually Max, and I went to sit. I stayed there, staring at my tea, and ultimately the cashier came to me to apologize for not asking for my name when she took the order. Her name was Destiny. You can't make that up.

I realized the fault did not come from her. Maybe yes, the coffee place should have had a process where they asked everyone's name instead of using the name on the credit card, but also, my brain started to function again. I got out of my panic moment: the app the cafe used to collect payment could have a separate field to input a name distinct from the name written on the credit card. This simple fix could have saved me this traumatic experience and the fear of direct violence for being outed as transgender in a public space.

I realized I could impact change and improve gender inclusion issues using my unique perspective in society and the Service Design workshops methodology I practiced for years as a startup designer. I saw how I could leverage the user research sessions and ideation workshops to focus on human-centered inclusion problems instead of profit-centered business problems. This call was impossible not to listen to: I felt the urge to use my superpowers and unique perspective to open people's minds to how risky a gendered society is.

I embraced that new power by using my voice to reach even more people and learning to stop talking to leave space for underrepresented voices. I decided to put my successful design company on hold and train teams to be more gender-inclusive by figuring out solutions in the products and services they release. This side project has been an enormous success. Someone shared that using some of my tips interested a university in placing a transgender student on their staff. We know how hard it is to find the first job, especially as an underrepresented person. Even just one transgender person having a more prosperous life means this is a success for me.

The excitement of this new adventure brought me back to the infinite energy I had in high school for the arts when I created projects all the time, day and night. I remember this goofy little guy I used to draw with short hair, jeans, and sneakers. I named him Max. I keep wondering how my life would have unfolded if a transgender person had actively helped me figure out my gender at the time. I want to be that person for a young Max.

As I allowed myself to live as authentically as possible and listen to my needs, I felt my confidence increase while my imposter syndrome felt less and less present.

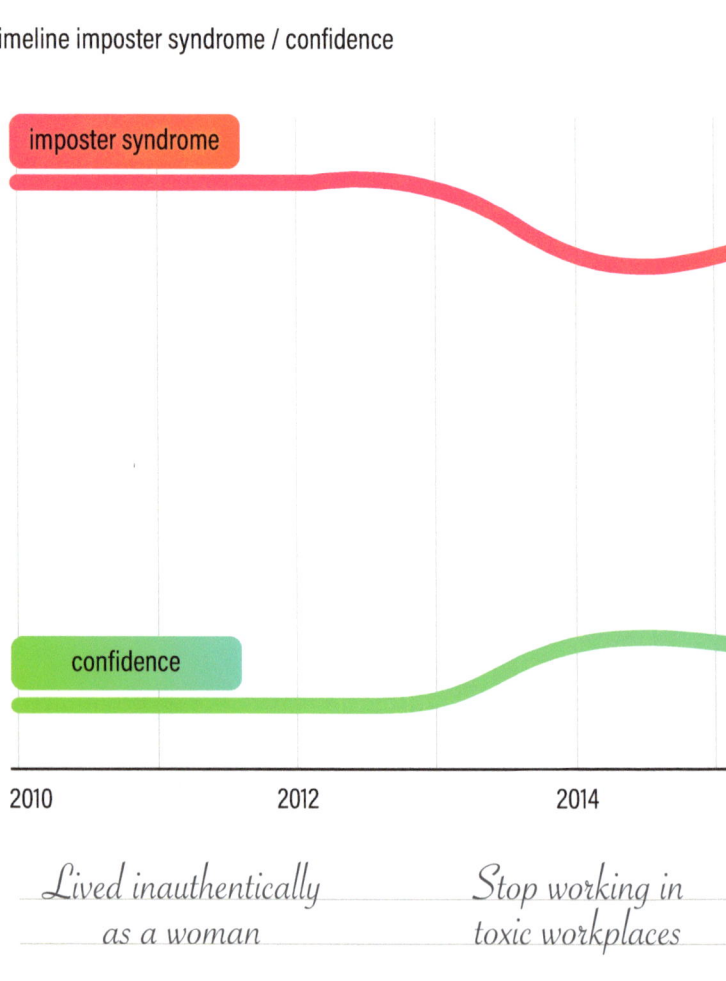

Timeline imposter syndrome / confidence

imposter syndrome

confidence

2010 · 2012 · 2014

Lived inauthentically as a woman

Stop working in toxic workplaces

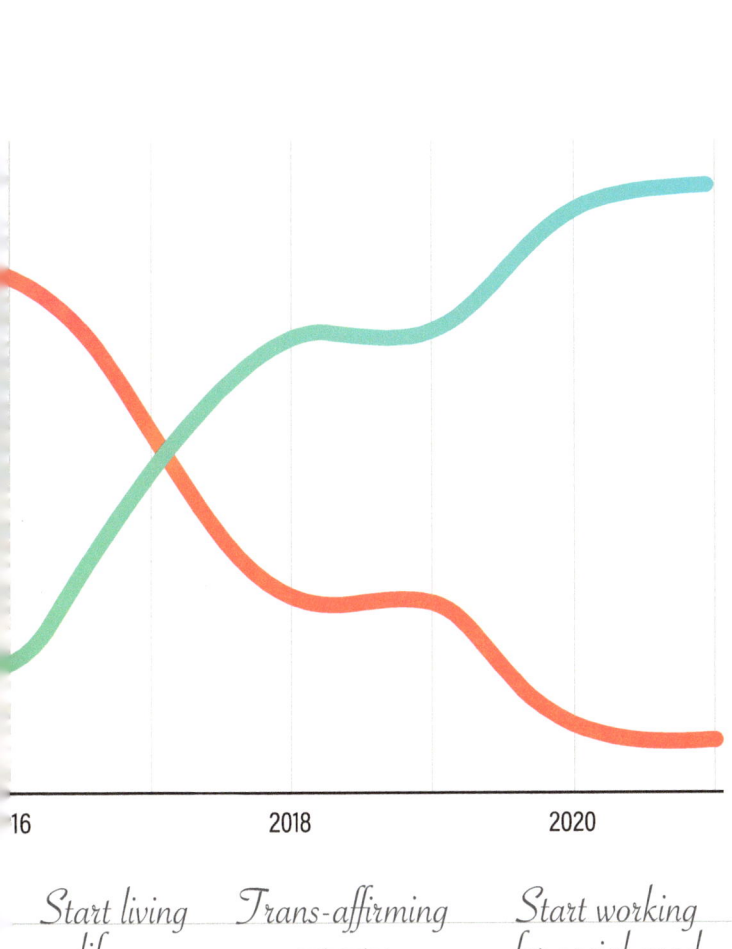

16   2018   2020

*Start living   Trans-affirming   Start working
my life as my   surgery   for social good
authentic self   companies*

Use this blank chart to assess your imposter syndrome and confidence levels over the past years. Pick a year and add the life details under the chart. Place a dot for your level of confidence. Put another dot for your sense of feeling imposter syndrome. When all done, trace two lines: one for your imposter syndrome and one for your confidence.

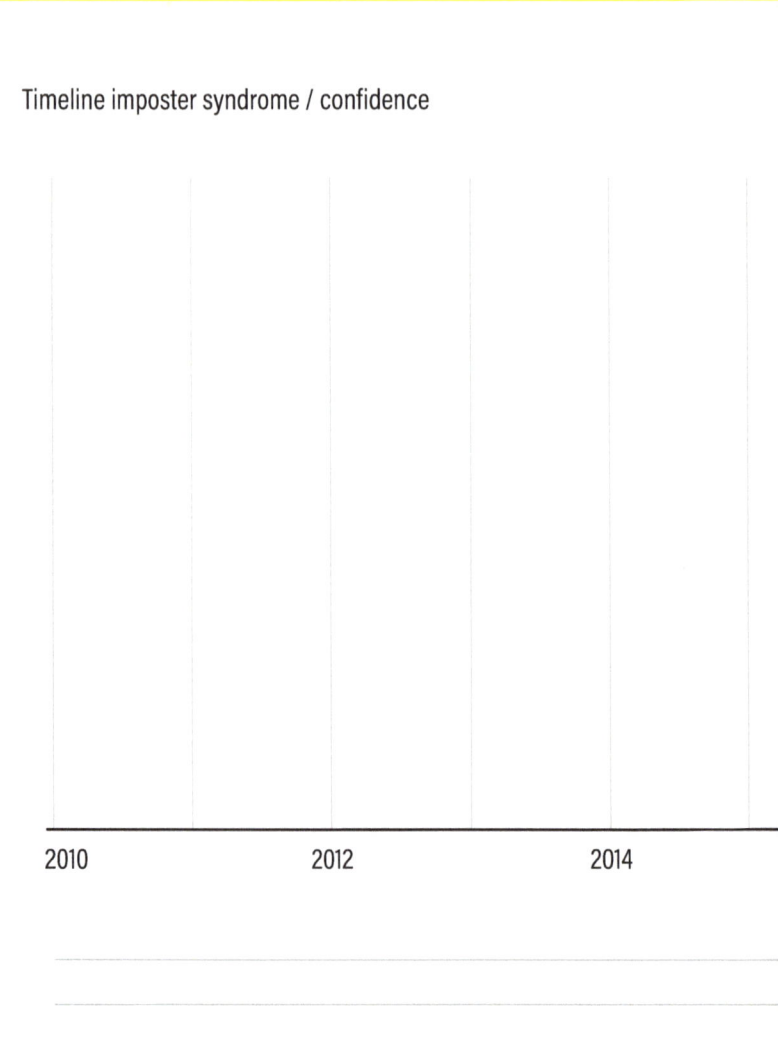

Timeline imposter syndrome / confidence

2010   2012   2014

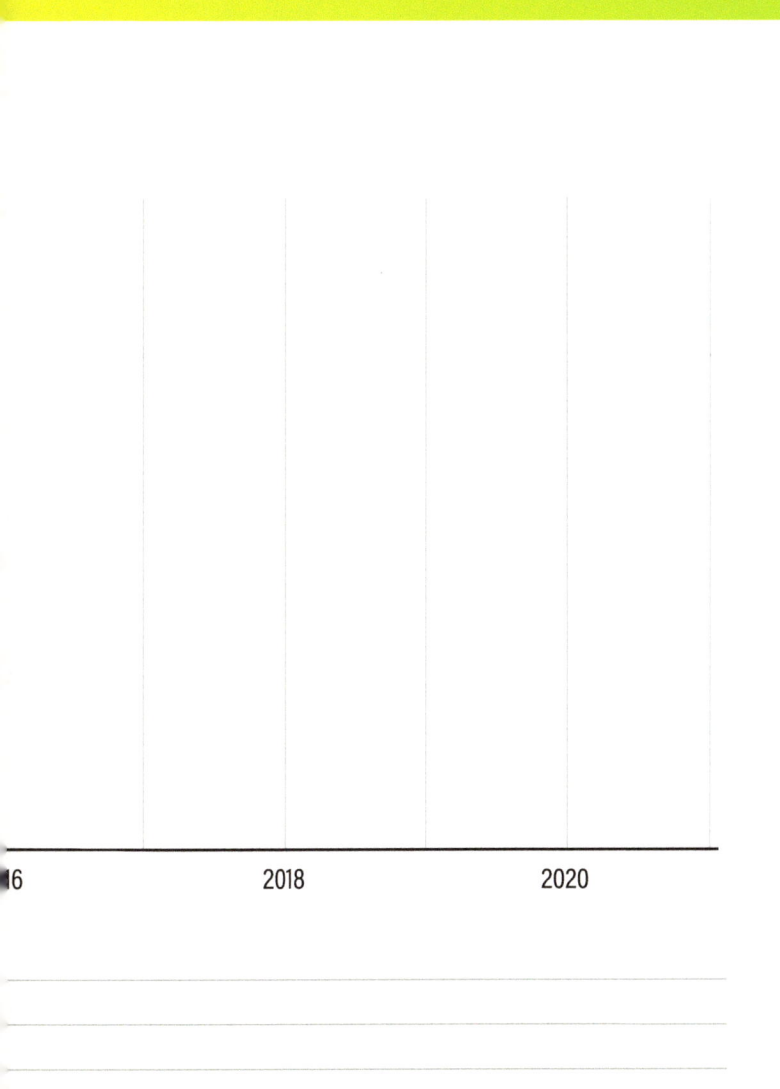

6   2018   2020

What did you notice? How did it make you feel?

What was surprising?

Let's thank ourselves for caring for our well-being and being honest with where we are. Facing our actual state is the first step toward change.

Now that we understand imposter syndrome better and how it connects with our identities, let's dig into each step to overcome imposter syndrome. We are going to start by listening to our needs and setting our boundaries.

LISTENING TO OUR NEEDS AND SETTING BOUNDARIES

Not Feeling Lonely in Solitude

I spent all my life being busy, always having to be with someone or be somewhere to the point of codependency, where I would manipulate people to change their plans so they would stay with me. I dreaded staying alone with myself. Loneliness was the scariest thing. I believe now that being by myself would have meant that I had to face who I was, and until I had the support around me, it felt too risky to look deeper.

Life feels like a thick fog when we feel disconnected from our bodies and do not align with how we present ourselves to the world. I lived with a constant lack of clarity regarding my needs, what I liked or disliked, who I should trust, which paths to take. In that context, imposter syndrome can grow very well and overcome a person.

Here are some of the feelings that were holding me back:

- Drowning in self-doubt

- Not being able to acknowledge, let alone celebrate my success

- Codependency on others to feel worthy

- Hating myself

- No inner power

- Feeling lost

- Chronic anxiety

- Not feeling that I do enough or that I am enough

It would show up in relationships where I would cut things short when I felt some lack of control. I would think that the other person wanted to hurt me emotionally, so I would break up before that could happen. This self-sabotaging cost me multiple relationships and a lot of remorse.

It started to change when I joined Codependent Anonymous (CoDA). In this 12-step program, we focus on codependency and live a healthier life without the need for others to validate ourselves.

I attended CoDA meetings a few times a week. Very quickly, I felt validated that my reactions and behaviors were coming from how I grew up. It took a couple of years to arrive at a point of healing where I could give love to my suffering. I forgave myself. I realized the harm that I have caused by letting my trauma and codependency take control over. I planned on making amends to those I hurt when I was still living on a reactional system.

Like my learning from meditation, I started to enjoy the quietness, make time, and welcome spaciousness. My codependency transformed itself into inner love and self-approval.

It gave me additional space to explore myself even more and face my trauma. In the middle of the Covid pandemic in 2020, I found the bravery to open a door that I had kept closed for all my adult life. I heard someone during a CoDA meeting talk about being part of Survivors of Incest Anonymous (SIA). I got interested in reading more about it, and everything I had forgotten for twenty-five years came back to me.

I joined SIA, and after the first meetings, I stayed in a ball on my bed, sobbing about how others' stories were similar to mine. It required some strength and mental force to finally speak about the repeated incest I endured from my teenage years to my young adult life.

I grew from reaching my most profound trauma. The incest does not control me anymore; it is not a secret anymore, something that I have to hide to protect my perpetrator. An excellent therapist supports me, and I've benefited from Eye Movement Desensitization and Reprocessing (EMDR) sessions for the past years, which changed my life. This therapeutic method allows us to safely access painful memories and reprogram them with the therapist's help. It is exceptionally efficient for Post Traumatic Stress Disorder when we cannot seem to stop replaying the memory in a loop.

Facing imposter syndrome requires mental health exploration and support. I am not a therapist, and I am just here to share my story. I encourage us to surround ourselves with professionals or groups when we feel that it is time to unlock those difficult moments of our past. We gain so much from being in control of our history. For me, with each step I took towards my truth, the more room I had in my mind to welcome new challenges and to face more layers of my identity. It is easier to overcome imposter syndrome when ghosts from our past do not inundate us.

More recently my psychiatrist diagnosed and treated me for bipolar disorder. The diagnosis brought clarity. It all made sense why I had high manic moments for a few days in a row, followed by deep depression days to the point that I did not remember what I was doing and for how long. For example, I worked on half of this book in just a few days in the summer of 2020, writing sticky notes by the dozens and putting them in my living room. I ended up with hundreds of them on my walls. Yes, that productivity was phenomenal, but also not healthy. I barely slept, followed by a week of being completely unmotivated, hit hard by imposter syndrome and self-doubt.

In the beginning, this book talked about inner power. It slowly became more evident after a few workshops that many people, if not everyone, experienced imposter syndrome. I initially struggled to find the best way to share my learnings practically while opening my story to inspire others to access their inner power. What's going to interest folks? Do people want to know about my personal life as a trans person, or do they only care about activities to grow their confidence?

It is impossible to separate the personal from work because how we feel about ourselves impacts how we present ourselves to the world, our teammates, managers, and clients.

A big piece of my growth happened in 2018 when

I had access to gender-affirming surgery: top surgery. As a transmasculine person, having a large chest since my teenage days always brought me discomfort and blocked me from fully living my best life. I used a binder to flatten my chest, even in the hot summer of NYC. For me, this physical transformation unlocked a mental health freedom.

On May 17, 2018, when I woke up from the top surgery, I instantly felt lighter. I described it as a deep sense of clarity on my identity and goals, having some brain fog swiped away. My inner power has grown nonstop since then.

Not all trans people want or have access to affirming surgery. I share only my own experience and my testimony on how my body and mind are interdependent.

Following this day, I became more assertive, and it made some friends walk away, not finding what they used to see in me. I grew to be less codependent, starting to say no more often, listening to my needs first. I learned to let go, pick myself over others, and embrace the grief of losing relationships that did not work anymore. I learned interdependence as a way of living in a community.

Interdependence is a more balanced way of seeing how we interact with others. The extremes are dependence, where we cannot exist without others, and independence, where we don't need anyone. Interdependence is the harmony where we rely on others when needed, and we also give to the community when others need it.

For that to exist, we need to know our needs and what our boundaries are.

BOUND
SELF

PARIES

LOVE

Our boundaries are crossed when someone does something that's off-limits. In the beginning it can be hard to identify our needs and limits. Let's practice setting our boundaries with this activity.

You are exhausted because you never stop working. You reply to all emails and messages you receive on evenings, weekends, and vacations. Your boss is asking for a document on a Saturday morning.

I will allow *to reply in a timely manner during work hours.*

I will tolerate *to work late sometimes if planned in advance.*

I will not allow *to be available on weekends and vacations.*

How we set our boundaries:

"Here is the document. Also, to preserve my health, I will stop replying to emails and Slack messages after 6pm or on weekends."

You welcomed a friend to stay at your place for a few nights, giving up your bed for them. It has been a week now, your back hurts from sleeping on the sofa, and you miss your privacy.

I will allow

I will tolerate

I will not allow

How we set our boundaries:

When you meet up with a friend after work, they barely say hi before dumping all their anxiety onto you by sharing how their day was terrible.

I will allow _____

I will tolerate _____

I will not allow _____

How we set our boundaries:

_____

_____

_____

Think about a situation that happened recently where you felt
uncomfortable or even disrespected. What did you notice?
How did you feel? Try to set your boundaries around this event.

I will allow

I will tolerate

I will not allow

How we set our boundaries:

What did you notice? How did it make you feel?

What is surprising?

Finding Ourselves And Our Boundaries

Boundaries are all about how we communicate our needs and what we do not accept. It is hard work, and it is worth it because the reward is receiving the respect we deserve.

Until my transition, I used to please people driven by a fear of being rejected. I used to adapt myself to others' needs or tastes -- lying about the music I liked to make sure people would like me, accept me. By my mid-twenties, I didn't even know what I wanted or who I really was— I had molded myself to a palatable version of myself.

It took me a lot of time to accept that being me won't please everyone: the affirming steps I took culminated when I walked into another therapist's office and shyly babbled, "I guess I am a boy." I guess I am me. I think I forgot about myself.

In the following months, I met some beautiful people in the trans community. Some became my chosen family and are still strong pillars in my everyday life. I grew into a more authentic version of myself, day by day.

Making choices became super easy, even in the tiny situation like just grabbing the cereal box at the supermarket with confidence, while I used to stay ten minutes in front of boxes of cereals, not knowing what I liked. That might sound trivial, but knowing what I wanted made me feel empowered. And it had a tremendous effect on my career. It's like meeting ourselves for the first time, discovering opinions, views, preferences, hobbies, new pleasures.

2018 marked the shift where I committed to using my skills as a service designer to build inclusive design workshops, primarily to support trans employees and trans customers.

I also became picky about the clients I wanted to work with, focusing on mission-driven companies. I worked for a few therapy and healthcare companies as well as civic startups.

For example, I supported Higher Ground Labs, led by Mollie Ruskin (she/her). I felt an immense honor to jump in and work with her. I've been admiring her work since I heard her talk about civic design in 2017. Listening to her presentation and how her work had impacted millions of people got me inspired to seek out civic projects. So when she called me, I felt a considerable boost in my confidence. I remember the moment of realization when I started the project and thought, Oh wait. I AM doing what I dreamed of in 2017.

If we make intentions of what we desire, it comes to reality. Yes, easy to say. But if we focus on our goal, it's easier to make decisions aligned with it. Between 2017 and the end of 2019, I shifted my work to inclusive design and shared my progress with the world. Mollie kept an eye on my work, and she showed some excitement to work with me. I didn't even know that she knew I existed.

During the time I worked with Mollie, I worked in therapy to accept the anger I kept inside. I learned at a young age that anger is wrong, and I have to keep my emotions to myself to be accepted.

It took a lot to feel and accept my anger. For the first six months, my therapist asked me what I felt and I had no answer. Nothing. My vocabulary and understanding of myself were minimal.

Why did accepting that I felt some anger take so long? My understanding now is that it meant breaking the protection of people-pleasing. It meant creating frictions with others and facing potential rejection for voicing my emotions, for being who I was.

It turned into a rebirth work that included mess and pain but it had to happen for me to exist as my authentic self.

I got a sidekick later with the influential book "Love & Rage" by Lama Rod Owens (he/him). I also took his online offerings and sat with my anger. Not avoiding it, not ignoring it, but listening to what it had to teach me. It opened a breakthrough around my childhood, my identity, and my need for boundaries.

It allowed me to feel the anger towards childhood abuse and the adults around me who closed their eyes and did not help or protect me.

Vetting Projects

The talented George Aye (he/him) is a significant teacher around boundaries. He co-runs the social good Greater Good Studio in Chicago with Sara Cantor (she/her). I had the privilege to attend some of his workshops, particularly his powerful Vetting Grid workshop. In just two hours, he completely shifted my relations with my clients. He inspired me to revise the unbalanced power dynamic where I saw myself as inferior to my clients. He dismantled the firm belief that capitalism is the only way to succeed, and only after that, I embraced the fact that I can make a living by working for/ with good people.

To achieve that goal, I had to decide to vet my clients and face the fear of saying no more often than yes to determine the worthy ones to support.

In the following exercise, we will focus on our latest proud achievements. We need to define what success means to us first. It can do a lot of different things, and it will look different for everyone. It could be that we got praise from a colleague, we got a new job or a promotion, or just the fact that we finished a task!

Take a moment to remember the projects (personal and professional) you worked on in the past 12 months. For each project, decide if it is one that you would not do again, or if you would gladly do again.

Organizing a birthday party		

Supporting low-income folks		

One project that I would not do again.

Organizing a birthday party

Reasons why it was not good

☐ *Timeline was too short*

☐ *Nobody listened to my ideas*

☐ *Had to handle lots of people*

☐

☐

This list makes me feel

Overwhelmed, invisible, rushed, stressed,

that I am not good enough

Hell no!

Needs for each issue that I had with this project

⇨ *I need projects with plenty of time*

⇨ *I need my ideas to be heard*

⇨ *I don't want to manage people*

⇨

⇨

This list makes me feel

Heard, valued, relaxed, in control

One project that I would not do again.

_____

Reasons why it was not good

☐ _____

☐ _____

☐ _____

☐ _____

☐ _____

This list makes me feel

_____

_____

Needs for each issue that I had with this project

⇨ _____

⇨ _____

⇨ _____

⇨ _____

⇨ _____

This list makes me feel

_____

_____

One project that I would do again

Project to support low-income folks

Reasons why it was good

☐ *My input was valued*

☐ *I saw the impact in the community*

☐ *I conducted interviews with folks*

☐

☐

This list makes me feel

Proud, grateful

Needs that were met with this project

⇒ *I need to be valued*

⇒ *I need projects with social impact*

⇒ *I need to interact with people*

⇒

⇒

This list makes me feel

Grounded, powerful, excited

One project that I would do again

Reasons why it was good

☐ _____

☐ _____

☐ _____

☐ _____

☐ _____

This list makes me feel

Needs that were met with this project

⇨ _____

⇨ _____

⇨ _____

⇨ _____

⇨ _____

This list makes me feel

_____

_____

In the first column, list all your needs from the previous pages.

Needs

I need to be valued

Step 1 - Listening to Our Needs and Setting Boundaries

Put your opportunities through your vetting grid to compare them with your needs. Put a checkmark when it aligns. If you don't know if it aligns, prepare a question you could ask the project team.

Project #1	Project #2	Project #3
✓	✓	☐
☐	☐	☐
☐	☐	☐
☐	☐	☐
☐	☐	☐
☐	☐	☐
☐	☐	☐
☐	☐	☐
☐	☐	☐
☐	☐	☐
☐	☐	☐

What is surprising?

_____

_____

_____

_____

_____

_____

_____

Does it align or not with how you felt with those projects?

we know our worth

Step 2

REIMAGINING WHO WE WANT TO BE

Society and how I grew up conditioned me to agree with authority figures, completely forgetting about my ideas, values, and even identity. When we have gaslighted ourselves for so long, meaning that we tell ourselves lies about who we are, it is difficult to get out of it without external support and tools to reimagine who we actually are.

As a parent, I work hard on making sure my kid has the space and freedom to explore who he is and how he wants to evolve as a teenager and young adult. My job is to keep him close to his inner power, making room for him to speak up, to voice his thoughts and beliefs by supporting him in maintaining alignment between his mind and body.

WE CAN
REINVENT
OURSELVES

When My Kid Told Me He Was a Boy

It happened at breakfast, between eating cereal and doing cartwheels. I answered, "Do you need my help to tell your friends that you are a boy today at school?"

He said, "Yep." Then he put on his usual basketball shorts, a colorful tee-shirt, a different shoe on each foot, and we walked to school.

That day he decided to use he/him pronouns.

He offered pronouns stickers to his friends in the classroom to show which pronoun they use. All the kids were very excited to wear their pronouns stickers proudly.

I realized that my kid leads a revolution only dreamed by his ancestors and trancestors, the trans people who were alive before us. When I look back at my family tree, I know where he got that strength.

My grandfather fought capitalism, signing petitions against supermarkets in France in the sixties. My dad's activism took shape by being part of the Communist Revolutionary Youth and proudly kicking racist people out of his office.

I never understood why their different yet similar activisms never aligned. I heard them fight often. Both were using their loud voices, sometimes hitting their fists on the table to make a point.

Well, one day in 1990, they couldn't fight anymore as my grandfather died in a hospital bed.

That happened in France, in Normandy, where I grew up. Every summer and family holiday, we would go to my grandparents' house with its big green backyard. My cousins and I would run around and climb trees until the darkness would come and an owl would sing.

Just before I turned eight, we all gathered again in that house for my grandfather's funeral. I didn't feel any sadness. I mostly felt bored.

Until I saw my dad cry. I saw this vulnerable part of him for the first time, and I felt scared, alone, unprotected. My dad would impress me so much that I would cry just addressing him at dinner. Yet, he would show up for me years later to fight for me to join an art school even though he dropped out of high school because everyone told him that he would never be good at anything.

But there, at thirty-four, in this church in Normandy, he cracked open.

I think that day, my dad realized that he hadn't had enough time with his dad to be seen for who he really is. Well, if my dad had died when I turned thirty-four, he would have never met my true self because I accepted my transness at thirty-five.

At thirty-five, I was a proud mom, visiting family in Melbourne, Australia, walking around pushing my kid in a blue Yoyo stroller, wearing my red summer dress and my large polka dot hat. It was so damn hot, and my annoying hair kept my head warm for no reason.

Trump just got elected, and I had some intense anger. When I sat down on the 1950's red leather hairstylist chair that day, I got the strength to ask for what I always wanted but never allowed myself to have: a very short haircut.

My thighs were sweating in the chair under the big black cape covering my body. The hairstylist cut my hair shorter and shorter, inch after inch. I stayed still the whole time.

I was looking at the mirror.

In the mirror.

I was looking into my own eyes.

And suddenly, I saw a glimpse of myself for the first time ever. My true self: I saw me, Max.

I didn't know yet, but that day, I sat down as Sophie, and I got up as Max.

It didn't feel like a coming out. It felt like a waking up. I wish I could say that at the moment everything felt perfect and I reached the happy ending of the story. But in reality, I felt terrified.

What did I see? Who did I just see? Who was I, really? An imposter? What was the truth? I had no clue and it confused me a lot.

After a couple of years looking for myself, I found my very own activism through gender inclusion, trans rights, and trans liberation. I battled on many levels but got rewarded when I discovered other ancestors I didn't know I had: the trans people who fought for me to live my life as a trans person myself. The trans people who fought for my kid so he could live his life as his authentic self.

Marsha P. Johnson, Sylvia Rivera. I call them my trancestors.

Thanks to them, my kid didn't have to come out. He had the freedom to explore his gender from day one. He just listened to his heart and knew he was a boy.

When a challenge comes up, we often feel afraid and stuck. What if we fail? Let's use the following activity to listen to our fears in order to not let them control us.

I am afraid to

Write and publish a book

Why?

I never published a book

Why?

I won't have enough time and it will take years

Why?

Real authors will laugh at my book

Fear can make our view very restricted. Rather than talking ourselves out of fear (very hard to do), we can choose to widen the view. Whether or not the fear is valid, I promise other things are true too. Spend some time exploring what else exists alongside the fear.

What else is true?

Next time, I won't be writing for the first time

What else is true?

I will have done something I have dreamed of

What else is true?

I chose courage in risk, better than being stuck

You Don't Suck

When a challenge comes up, we often feel afraid and stuck. What if we fail? Let's use the following activity to listen to our fears in order to not let them control us.

I am afraid to

_____

Why?

_____

Why?

_____

Why?

_____

Fear can make our view very restricted. Rather than talking ourselves out of fear (very hard to do), we can choose to widen the view. Whether or not the fear is valid, I promise other things are true too. Spend some time exploring what else exists alongside the fear.

What else is true?

What else is true?

What else is true?

What did you notice? How did it make you feel?

What was surprising?

Leading a Revolution

My kid is now seven, still a boy wearing colorful clothes and dancing to Katy Perry's songs. Some people are still using she/her pronouns for him. I ask him what he wants to do about it. I see his inner power when he answers, "Maybe we can just ignore them?" He knows his truth; he knows his worth.

My kid leads his own revolution by being his true self. By refusing to be misgendered, he teaches his grandparents a new level of love and acceptance, which allows them to accept me more fully.

My child is the most powerful person he can be. I don't know what transness and queerness will be for people like him, who could be themselves from birth, but I know he is not alone.

He has me and all his ancestors and trancestors' powers in his veins.

I grew up in France, where the culture relies heavily on appearances. Since I can remember, my body received comments that I never welcomed or requested. From the size of my body to the way I dressed. Even as a grown-up adult, I still received comments on what I wore from my parents.

It became a fundamental boundary I had to set with my parenting, "We don't talk about other people's bodies." Period. I surround myself with folks who value this as well. Where we support and respect each other.

In this large community, I count Shoog McDaniel (they/them). They probably don't know about me, but I admire them. They take powerful and magical pictures of fat queer folks, some of them underwater. They are breathtaking.

I have their pictures hanging on my walls, and my kid always likes to look at them, these free bodies.

When I challenged myself by adding diverse people to my Instagram, I discovered them — I started to follow bigger folks, more Black individuals, more Indigenous, People of Color, more people with disabilities. Changing what we see every day transforms our minds and biases.

I work through the discomfort of seeing different perspectives, opposite what society glorifies. Those beautiful people who didn't know me made me believe in beauty in bodies. I fell in love with my own body over the years just by changing my Instagram feed content. We cannot be who we cannot see. What we watch and digest has a profound impact on what we value and how we view ourselves.

Shoog helped me heal from the body police I grew up around, and they also support my kid into growing up as a free human being, happy in their body and proud of how they look. At five, while we were visiting my parents in France, he proudly reminded them that we don't talk about other people's bodies.

I do feel like I am healing generational trauma by being who I am, by raising a free and gender-expansive kid.

Another fundamental person I follow on Instagram is Jonah Welch (they/them). Some of their art is around the sentence "Trans people are sacred." When I met Jonah a couple of years ago, they traveled through New York with their van, and I offered my place for them to rest for a few days. I observed them in awe making art every day, even on the corner of my crowded desk. They made me believe in art again. In the power of art. Healing art.

That same year, I also stepped into art-making, doing

a challenging new adventure: dancing. By growing my confidence in my body through my transition, I had a stronger sense of groundedness and more power to utilize. I never really danced, convinced that I couldn't move my arms and legs gracefully, listening to my imposter syndrome way too much for fear of being ridiculed.

It all started when I attended an improv dance show by the Russian dance company Vozdukh Center of Physical Theatre by Anastasia Vorobyeva (she/her). They were asking the audience to share a personal story, and they were dancing it. Even the intimidation I felt did not stop me from gathering the courage to share my story of coming out as trans. And they danced the pains in my childhood of not feeling like I belonged, the difficulties in adapting, and the grief.

I watched them, and I cried. The dancers acted with their movements so powerfully, exactly connecting with the feelings I had inside my heart.

I jumped in and decided to do the workshop they were offering the following day. I discovered that I could dance and express emotions with my body. I did not know at the time that a few months later I would join a professional dance company for a summer workshop where I felt welcomed and valued in my art of dancing. I learned that jumping into the unknown and taking a risk will always pay off for me.

WE
ARE OUR
AUTHENTIC
SELF WHEN
WE ARE
ALIGNED
WITH OUR
INNER POWER

Sometimes what we are spending energy on does not match the goals we have. As you consider your definition of "success" how does that align with your time and energy outputs now?
Is there anything you could shift in order to move yourself into closer alignment between goals and day-to-day life?

Envision yourself in a year. You achieved your goals and you are the most successful you've ever been.

You can close your eyes for a few minutes to really experience this moment.

What did you notice? What did you accomplish?

_____

_____

_____

_____

In a year, I will

Imagine we travel through time and we discover it failed.

It failed because

- [ ] _____
- [ ] _____
- [ ] _____
- [ ] _____
- [ ] _____
- [ ] _____
- [ ] _____
- [ ] _____

Actions I can take today to avoid the failure in the future

⇨ _____

⇨ _____

⇨ _____

⇨ _____

⇨ _____

⇨ _____

⇨ _____

⇨ _____

What did you notice? How did it make you feel?

What was surprising?

Taking Risks

In 2020, I tried an app to learn how to play the piano. I always wanted to learn, but it never happened. I didn't play music or sing during my childhood. Therefore, I assumed that I couldn't sing, play music, or dance. I believed that I was not good. My imposter syndrome discouraged me from even trying.

Learning with the app on my phone brought so much joy and a rewarding feeling that I decided to get a keyboard and improve. It surprised me that I was not that bad, that I could learn a new skill. It unlocked something in me, something profound, something that wanted to get out. When we follow what feels good instead of avoiding what might feel bad, like shame, we grow faster and healthier.

Learning how to play the piano led to another step. I took a unique course about trans voices by Orion S. Johnstone (they/he). I explored how to find my voice as a trans person, and I allowed myself to be loud and be heard. It terrified me to take the classes. It took me five sessions to even dare to sing one line of a song, the shame of singing and not being good overwhelming me. After the seventh class, I finally built the love for my voice, the shame and guilt were now minimal, and I reached what I signed up for, singing in front of folks. They all shared moving compliments after my song. I copied them on a document to reread them later, multiple times.

My imposter syndrome kept telling me that they were lying, that they were just kind. Even now I have some self-doubt. But what I am sure of is how I felt, whatever the quality of it. Orion, my teacher, offered some deep healing work by supporting me in finding my voice.

More often than not, jumping into discomfort and running towards what is scaring us is the way to go. I won't become a singer who has live concerts, that's not what I mean. But it gave me more confidence in many aspects of my life, personal life, and work life. I don't suck. I am capable of great things. We don't suck. We are capable of great things. Nothing is set in stone.

Writing this book challenged my imposter syndrome so much. This is the first book I am writing and every week I feel like I am out of my league and someone will show up and laugh at me, at my writing. But I remind myself that releasing this beautiful book into the world will impact some lives, that my book is needed.

TAKING RISKS = GROWTH

ACCESSING OUR INNER POWER

Waking Up

Early in my career, I worked at a startup.

As we started a completely new product in a new market, I suggested that we run a few usability testings to understand what people would enjoy or not in our prototype. It came from the concern I had that we would build a very sophisticated service that would not match what the audience needed.

I ended up believing the Creative Director when he said that he/we didn't "believe" in usability testing. I did not challenge his belief. I trusted him because of him being my mentor.

Challenging his thoughts would have meant that I might disappoint him, jeopardizing my job.

But what was his legitimacy to be the authority in user experience and usability testing decisions?

When I witnessed our failed launch, I wondered. After a year of working days and nights and on weekends, we just had to conclude that we built a service that did not match what our audience needed. Nobody showed interest in our innovative product.

After the disappointing launch, it got even more stressful. We had to rush to pivot and rebuild a new solution within weeks: even less sleep, less time to make skillful decisions.

I yielded to oppression, to pressure. I agreed with every decision forced on me. I lived in scarcity by being dependent on others' approval and letting them decide what my life would be.

Overwhelmed by self-doubt and overthinking about external approval, I couldn't hear my self-judgment, even less believe it.

I compared myself to this Creative Director for many years as he mentored me, seeking his approval for everything to the point that I walked away from my inner power; it faded more and more, like a glass covering a flame until it dies.

In the following activities, we will learn to resist the toxic culture of rushing, only caring about the outcome, and apologizing too often.

We need time to make skillful decisions. Our brain needs time to adapt to new content. We learned that producing quickly and meeting unrealistic deadlines is the only viable success. Let's challenge that and find other metrics of success.

My metrics of success

☐ *Learned a new skill*

☐ *Impacted people*

☐ *Made time for myself*

☐ _____

☐ _____

☐ _____

☐ _____

☐ _____

Let's practice honoring time for ourselves by answering people more thoughtfully without apologizing so often.

Apologies I often say

☐ *Sorry I am late.*

☐ *Sorry, I'll change this right now.*

☐ *Sorry, I don't know*

☐ _____

☐ _____

☐ _____

☐ _____

This list makes me feel

_____

_____

Honoring myself and others

⇨ *Thank you for waiting for me.*

⇨ *Thanks for your feedback.*

⇨ *I'll think about it and get back to you.*

⇨

⇨

⇨

⇨

This list makes me feel

DO
THEY
IGNITE
ME?

In order to cultivate our inner power, we need to surround ourselves with people who ignite our inner power and make it grow. Let's learn who we should spend more time with.

People I spend most of my time

- [ ]
- [ ]
- [ ]
- [ ]
- [ ]
- [ ]
- [ ]
- [ ]

One person I spend most of my time with

After meeting with them, I feel

- [ ] _____
- [ ] _____
- [ ] _____
- [ ] _____
- [ ] _____

Energized, fired up, excited

Tired, depleted, down

Detox From Oppressive Systems

When others' expectations or oppressive systems intoxicate us, we lose clarity about what we think. We become a tool for someone else's goal and inadvertently betray our own goals.

Many years later, I realized that I already had enough knowledge about usability testing at the beginning of the project, thanks to the many readings and conferences I attended. I did not trust myself to speak up and advocate to test our proof of concept. I complied and dismissed my own belief. I fawned, which turned into a pattern of people-pleasing and conflict avoidance driven by fear of being fired.

In the following years, I detoxed from suffocating my inner power by starting the vital process of (re)building my self-trust.

Sometimes quitting a job is the best thing we can do for ourselves. It took me many years to accept that I left a startup just before it grew big. The working conditions were unhealthy, and I lacked respect from some leaders. When I got the opportunity for other clients, I left and did not look back.

Well, that's not true. I beat myself up as I saw the company grow over the years, without me in it. What if I had stayed and sucked it up? Maybe by now, I would have had good equities? I struggled to let go and be confident that I made the right choice. At the time, I valued my well-being so little that I did not see how there was only one choice. I had to pick myself.

Thankfully, this self-doubt disappeared when many years later, I met an employee of that company who confessed that the culture there showed some toxicity and unethical practices. I would have suffered so much, my imposter syndrome would have skyrocketed, and it would have been harder to find my inner power in those conditions.

It confirmed my radar and how I could have trusted my guts back then.

Honoring our inner power means we speak our truth. We suffocate our inner power when we stay silent. Let's shape alternative futures by role modeling what is possible while resisting injustice.

Unfair situation I witnessed

☐ *A colleague makes a sexist joke*

☐ *Someone doesn't use the correct pronouns for a friend*

☐ *Having only one Black person in a team*

☐

☐

Speaking up means I could say

⇨ *I've heard your joke, and I don't think this is appropriate.*

⇨ *Reed is using they/them pronouns. I am not sure you were aware.*

⇨

⇨

⇨

Trusting Ourselves

That's how I entered into new positions moving forward—trusting my guts and my experience to make good decisions for myself. When I started a new design research job, I found the importance of ethical design in my manager. We fought side by side against the leadership's pushback, which led to not renewing my contract. I appeared as a troublemaker by advocating for inclusive design.

I find it captivating that people who challenge the status quo are labeled troublemakers. Who is labeling them? The people in power probably don't want to have less power by a potential shift in the status quo.

At the time, I still believed that authority figures knew more and better than me. When I did not get renewed, it felt like a failure after many months of hard work and advocacy.

However, when I learned that my manager quit just one month after I left, it confirmed my instincts. Maybe he hoped for change and an honest mission-driven company? For me, it meant that I did good by challenging leadership and authority to do better, even if that meant losing some contracts. I knew I did something right if people in power felt uncomfortable. I did not know yet, but I also impacted coworkers.

A few months later, another person quit, and we had a chat on how my inclusive design advocacy made him realize that he wanted to move towards more advocacy work. We can never overestimate the impact we have on folks around us. Being our authentic selves and being assertive about our integrity pays off in the long run. For me, that means speaking up and risking my position.

I have the privilege of being white with no college debt (I grew up in France, where I went to college for free. Yes, $0.). And I am here to use that power. If I lose a job, it is easier for me to bounce back than other folks. I have to use this to create change.

FEAR IS WISDOM

Visualize a time in the recent past when you felt a sense of uneasiness with someone in a position of authority (whether you felt a strong inner no or a subtle discomfort with a decision). Let's first identify the obstacle(s).

Last time I felt uncomfortable with someone in position of authority was when

If I speak up, I am afraid that

Let's build our resilience toolkit before the next interaction. Creating a plan in preparation for these moments can help us begin to break the cycle and unlearn patterns where we shut down when facing authority. Hint: It's all about preparation and *the pause*.

Fear

☐ If I speak up *my boss will think I'm a troublemaker*

☐ If I speak up

☐ If I speak up

☐ If I speak up

☐ If I speak up

Why it's worth the risk

▷ Even if *they think I'm a troublemaker*
I will *feel strong and proud*

▷ Even if _____
I will _____

▷ Even if _____
I will _____

▷ Even if _____
I will _____

▷ Even if _____
I will _____

It can be easier to practice boundaries setting with supportive people first. Let's identify them.

Safe people I can practice my boundaries with

- [ ] _____
- [ ] _____
- [ ] _____
- [ ] _____
- [ ] _____

I can ask them to be an ally in this practice by

- [ ] *Encouraging me to speak up* _____
- [ ] _____
- [ ] _____
- [ ] _____

WE ARE NOT ALONE

The best way to lead a conversation is to come prepared with clarity and confidence. Let's prepare alone or with our supportive people.

The most important point that I need to be heard

- [ ] _____
- [ ] _____
- [ ] _____
- [ ] _____
- [ ] _____
- [ ] _____
- [ ] _____
- [ ] _____

Go to phrases if I am not being heard

☐ _____

☐ _____

☐ _____

☐ _____

☐ _____

☐ _____

☐ _____

☐ _____

Let's reflect on our learning after the conversation with a person in a position of authority.

When I spoke up, I felt

_____

_____

_____

_____

What helped me

☐ _____

☐ _____

☐ _____

☐ _____

☐ _____

What was not helpful

- [ ]
- [ ]
- [ ]
- [ ]
- [ ]

I learned

Next time I speak up I will

BEING SILENT
MEANS OUR
INNER POWER
DIES LIKE A
FLAME UNDER
A GLASS.

What did you notice? How did it make you feel?

_____

_____

_____

_____

_____

_____

What was surprising?

Speaking Up

Later in my career, a company refused to acknowledge their lack of diversity in People of Color and LGBTQIA+ folks. My user research showed that they needed to hire more Black folks, People of Color, and queer and trans folks to serve their audience. Even with this data, they did not change their launch. However, they suddenly announced free services for Black folks right after the murder of George Floyd. I was long gone by then as they also saw me as a troublemaker.

Early in my career, I had to implement what a marketing team decided, driven by money over people's needs. Sadly, the role of a designer does not seem to include ethics.

We need to remember that integrity is everything. The view of others cannot take away the truth that a person acted in line with their integrity.

Authority and Feedback

When "Ruined by Design: How Designers Destroyed the World, and What We Can Do to Fix It" by Mike Monteiro (he/him) came out, it hit right at the core of what has bothered me since I started working in tech in 2008. I convinced myself that I was doing something wrong, that I was wrong, by thinking differently from my clients and my managers. I felt like I did not belong for thinking about ethical and community-centered design, even though we were not using those words yet. At the same time, everyone else focused on Return On Investment, raising millions of dollars, building and shipping quickly, dismissing edge cases and people with disabilities. Reading the book, I finally felt less alone!

It helped me see a vision of me saying no to unethical expectations—a version of myself trusting my inner power.

It showed me WHY we, designers and makers of technologies, should care about the design decisions we made and still make. How we have more power than we think, and we do not use it enough.

Collective growth happens with individual growth. We need more people to say no to unethical products and services. But how do we find the strength and courage, the bravery to say no?

Depending on the situation, we cannot always speak up and say no. We might not have the luxury of being able to switch job right at this moment for example. Honoring ourselves by realizing that a job does not match our needs anymore is already a strong discovery. The more we stay involved in an unhealthy dynamic, the more our imposter syndrome increases. We need to surround ourselves with supportive people or find them in different communities.

We might not be able to change the systemic issues by ourselves but we can prepare for an exit strategy to protect ourselves. Refreshing our resume with the help of a friend, applying to jobs, sharing around us that we are looking for a new position.

Knowing when to step away is wisdom and it's far from giving up. It's respecting and believing in ourselves.

In 2020, in the middle of the COVID pandemic, I decided to take Mike Monteiro's "Presenting with Confidence" workshop. At the time, I felt weak when I had to share my insights and use my voice loud and clear. I had a mindset where everyone else was right, and I didn't do enough to prove that my work was good enough.

I still hear Mike Monterio telling me, "Max, you are abused at work" when I shared the feedback I received from a manager after they did not renew my contract. It shocked me to hear those words and how quickly Mike saw the situation clearly. I genuinely believed the manager, who was not a design expert. I replayed the situation and realized that pushing for inclusive design might have annoyed him to the point of letting me go to avoid being challenged. Some people don't like to feel uncomfortable.

I suddenly had clarity on who I see as an authority and if they are equipped to give me skillful feedback. Whose opinions and leadership do we value and see as worthy of our respect? I moved away from my previous mindset, where anyone's opinion seemed to matter more than my own. I showed more assertiveness on who I trust, who I want to work with, and whose work I want to support.

I landed a new client the week of that workshop, after using the public speaking skills I learned from the workshop, but most importantly, after it swiped away more layers of my imposter syndrome.

INTEGRITY IS EVERYTHING

Sometimes, without realizing it, we are giving up our power. We get used to not being respected. Let's build our power back by checking our rights.

My own bill of rights

☐ I have a right to be invited to important meetings that impact my work

☐ I have a right to feel like my opinion is welcomed by people in power

☐ I have a right to have people listen without interrupting

☐ I have a right to feel like my authentic self at work

☐ I have a right to fair access to promotions and raises

☐ I have a right to feel allowed to disagree

☐ *I have a right to* _____

☐ *I have a right to* _____

☐ *I have a right to* _____

Did I have trouble believing some of these? Why?

Before asking for feedback, we should pause to become clear on the type of feedback that would be helpful to us and who would be equipped to help us.

Feedback I need

- [ ] _____
- [ ] _____
- [ ] _____
- [ ] _____
- [ ] _____
- [ ] _____
- [ ] _____
- [ ] _____

Who I should ask

- [ ] _____
- [ ] _____
- [ ] _____
- [ ] _____
- [ ] _____
- [ ] _____
- [ ] _____
- [ ] _____

Being precise on the type of feedback we are seeking will help us receive constructive advice.

As you are *part of the marketing team*
I'd like your feedback on *the campaign's call to action.*

As you are
I'd like your feedback on

As you are
I'd like your feedback on

As you are
I'd like your feedback on

As you are
I'd like your feedback on

As you are
I'd like your feedback on

As you are
I'd like your feedback on

As you are
I'd like your feedback on

Awakening Myself and Others

My purpose in life is to wake up others and create rituals for me and others. I learned this about myself by doing the Turtle Tank Leadership programs by Samia Abou-Samra (they/them) and Ije Ude (she/her).

It took the shape of a few weeks of self-discovery and learning how we function, mapping ourselves into the intuitive way of nature, how a caterpillar turns into a cocoon to become a butterfly. We all go through stages of highly creative moments, chaos, grief periods, wisdom, and growth. Understanding this cyclic pattern gave me a lot of spaciousness to listen to my inner power. It is a solid answer to the rushed pace white supremacy and capitalism make us follow. Let's take our time!

Awakening others is my core purpose, and you hold in your hands the outcome of this revelation from a few years ago: this workbook as well as the coaching and webinar sessions I host.

In the following exercise, we will focus on our latest proud achievements. We need to define what success means to us first. It can do a lot of different things, and it will look different for everyone. It could be that we got praise from a colleague, we got a new job or a promotion, or just the fact that we finished a task!

I want to support us in tapping into our inner power and finding our purpose. There won't be mystical prophecies: we already know, but we forgot.

Find something you feel proud of, a goal you reached, a difficult task you completed.

My recent success

How did you manage to reach that success?
Was it because of people you worked with? Because of a skill you
learned? Something you accomplished beforehand?

Step 1. How I achieved my success

How did you manage to reach step 1?
Was it because of people you worked with? Because of a skill you learned?
Something you accomplished beforehand?

Step 2. How I achieved the previous step (step 1)

How did you manage to reach step 2?
Was it because of people you worked with? Because of a skill you learned? Something you accomplished beforehand?

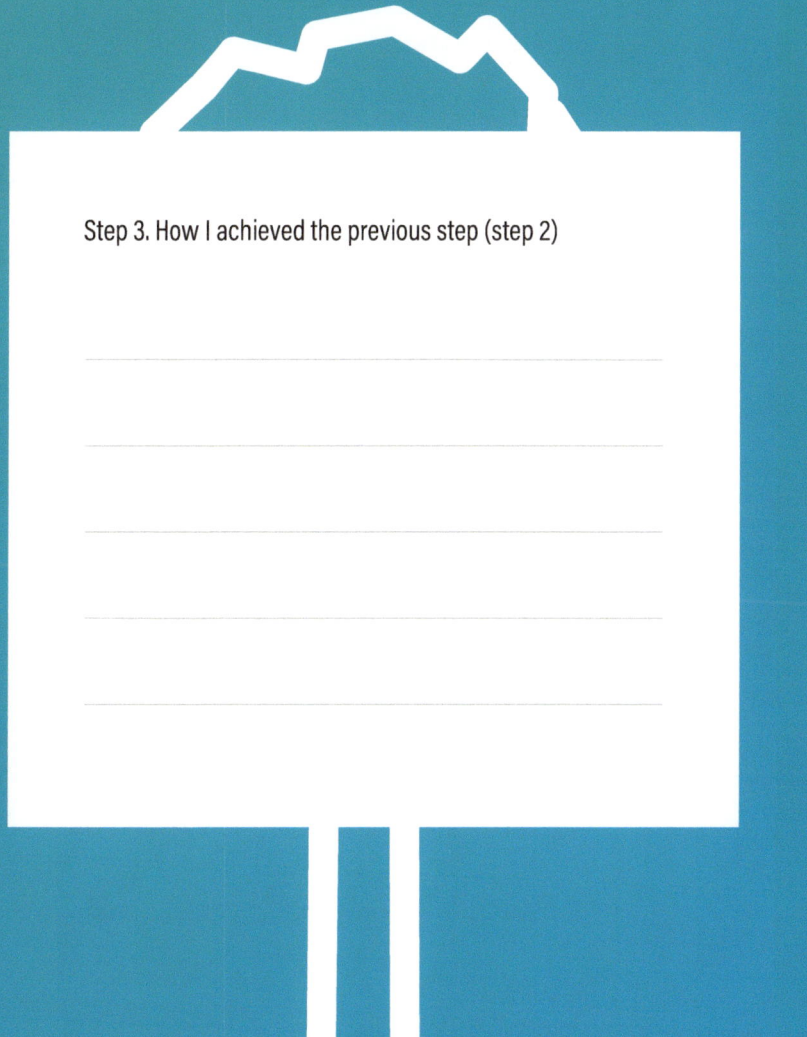

Step 3. How I achieved the previous step (step 2)

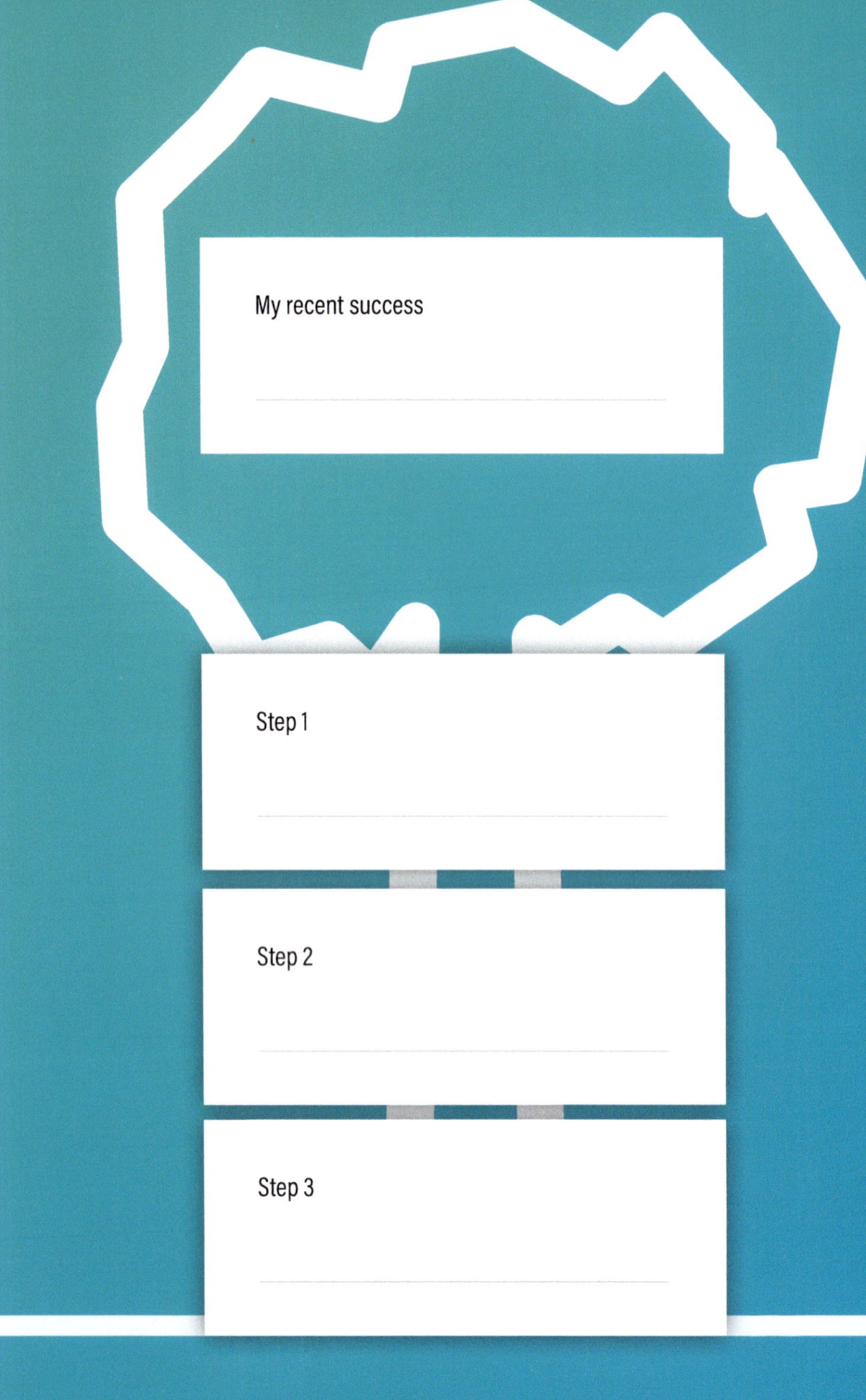

My recent success

Step 1

Step 2

Step 3

I successfully did

_____

_____

_____

_____

Because I did

_____

_____

_____

_____

What did you notice? How did it make you feel?

_____

_____

_____

_____

_____

_____

What was surprising?

_____

_____

_____

_____

_____

_____

FINDING OUR INTERDEPENDENT COMMUNITY

When I think about the term "Interdependent Community," I instantly remember this decisive moment I experienced with one hundred people who held me while I stepped into my inner power.

During a three-day silent meditation retreat for queer folks, I met two dharma teachers who became pillars into my queerness and meditation practice: Lama Rod (he/him) and La Sarmiento (they/them).

"Waking Up Fabulous" was the name of the retreat. And yes, I woke up fabulous.

We ended the last day by voicing what blossomed in us during the retreat. When I nervously took the microphone, I wondered if I had the right to speak up. If what I had to say would be useless.

During this retreat, I reached my inner self and gained the strength to say out loud, "Yes, I am a transmasculine person, and yes, I gave birth to my child. I am ready to stop thinking that I should not be proud of this because cisgender people feel uncomfortable when they imagine a masculine-presenting person being pregnant. F*ck their comfort. I won't hide that I gave birth to my child anymore."

I needed to hear my voice say those words. I needed to hear everyone clapping and smiling at me. So yes, I woke up fabulous, and I left healed and empowered AF.

Until that moment, I had imposter syndrome around my parenting. I kept hiding the fact that I gave birth to my child for fear of how others would perceive me, fear of being outed as a trans person and being seen as weird. Neither a mom nor a dad, I felt like a parent. Yet, I did not want to remove the powerful experience that giving birth is. This step into my authentic self brought me closer to my truth, and I became more powerful. And this is when my imposter syndrome faded away.

Meditation also helped me to step into my truth and remove some of the fear. My first meditation retreat happened a couple of months before. I got pulled in to attend a few days with a Queer Black woman teacher, Leslie Booker (she/her).

From her teaching, I discovered the metā practice that carried me through healing, forgiveness, and compassion for those who hurt others, who hurt me.

I experienced being in silence with myself for the first time, guided by Booker's kind and supportive work, as well as the other participants. I realized how silence is a friend to me and helps me feel grounded, really listening to my own needs and perspective.

I understood that we live in a system designed to overwhelm us by forcing us to work at a rushed pace, leading to burnout. I made silence, space, and time my new tools to thrive. "I can always create space" became my mantra. I started to resist the urgency that is imposed on us by white supremacy's oppressive standards. Resting became my antidote to oppressive systems.

We can always create space, even when we feel we are stuck. Changing small habits can ignite an increase in empowerment and even impact others around us. With this activity we will discover where to begin.

List a recent moment where you felt **anxious, pressured, or overwhelmed.**

During a meeting I quickly joined right after another one, I got caught off guard with a question.

I fumbled a quick answer that didn't satisfy me.

Why I felt anxious, pressured, or overwhelmed

☐ *I did not have time to prepare*

☐ *I felt pressured to reply in the moment*

☐ *I have too many meetings*

☐ _____

☐ _____

"Let me think about it and I'll get back to you."

New habits to create

⇨ *Plan my meetings to be fifty-five minutes*

⇨ *Reply, "I'll get back to you."*

⇨ *Plan a day each week without meetings*

⇨ _____

⇨ _____

List a recent moment where you felt **anxious, pressured, or overwhelmed.**

_____

_____

_____

Why I felt anxious, pressured, or overwhelmed

- [ ] _____
- [ ] _____
- [ ] _____
- [ ] _____
- [ ] _____

New habits to create

$\Rightarrow$ _____

$\Rightarrow$ _____

$\Rightarrow$ _____

$\Rightarrow$ _____

$\Rightarrow$ _____

We are now going to focus on moments where we felt empowered.

List a recent moment where you felt **relaxed, proud, or empowered.**

I received an email at 7pm and I decided to wait until the next morning to reply to it. By then, I had time to chat with a colleague and answer better to my manager.

Why I felt relaxed, proud, or empowered

- [ ] *I had time to think*
- [ ] *I did not spend my evening on emails*
- [ ] *I came back with a thoughtful answer*
- [ ] _____
- [ ] _____

"Please note I will never expect a reply from anyone during their chosen holidays."

New habits to create

⇨ *Breathe before answering an email*

⇨ *Create space for others by role modeling*

⇨ *Add an auto-response to wait 1-3 days*

⇨ _____

⇨ _____

List a recent moment where you felt **relaxed, proud, or empowered.**

_____

_____

_____

Why I felt relaxed, proud, or empowered

☐ _____

☐ _____

☐ _____

☐ _____

☐ _____

New habits to create

⇨ _____

⇨ _____

⇨ _____

⇨ _____

⇨ _____

What is surprising?

How did you feel?

Resting

Resting is an act of resistance and rebellion in a capitalist, productivity-based society.

Rest as resistance is the motto of The Nap Ministry, an organization founded in 2016 by Tricia Hersey (she/her) where they give space and time for folks to just rest. And breathe.

I remember reading a story about someone sleeping in a very silent desert. They started to be scared when they heard a "boom, boom, boom." It turns out they were able to hear their own heartbeat.

When we make space and we rest, we open the door to listen to ourselves and to access our true selves. We can listen to our emotions and we can answer to what happens to us in a more thoughtful way, instead of reacting over and over again. Space and time are two crucial elements in our liberation from imposter syndrome.

In the following activity, I will guide us into finding our comfort zone and how we can identify where we need support.

Before we can ask for support, we need to know which tasks we are dreaming of accomplishing, which goals we hope we can reach one day.

Activities that are **easy to do for me**

- [ ]
- [ ]
- [ ]
- [ ]
- [ ]
- [ ]
- [ ]

This list makes me feel

Activities and goals I wish I could do but **seem difficult**

- [ ]
- [ ]
- [ ]
- [ ]
- [ ]
- [ ]
- [ ]

Support I can ask

Activities and goals that seem **impossible to reach**

- [ ] _____
- [ ] _____
- [ ] _____
- [ ] _____
- [ ] _____
- [ ] _____
- [ ] _____

People who can help me

_____

_____

Visualizing our goals, even if they feel unreachable, is what will fuel us in the future. Here is mine from 2018, with writing a book in the "impossible to do". Yet, here we are!

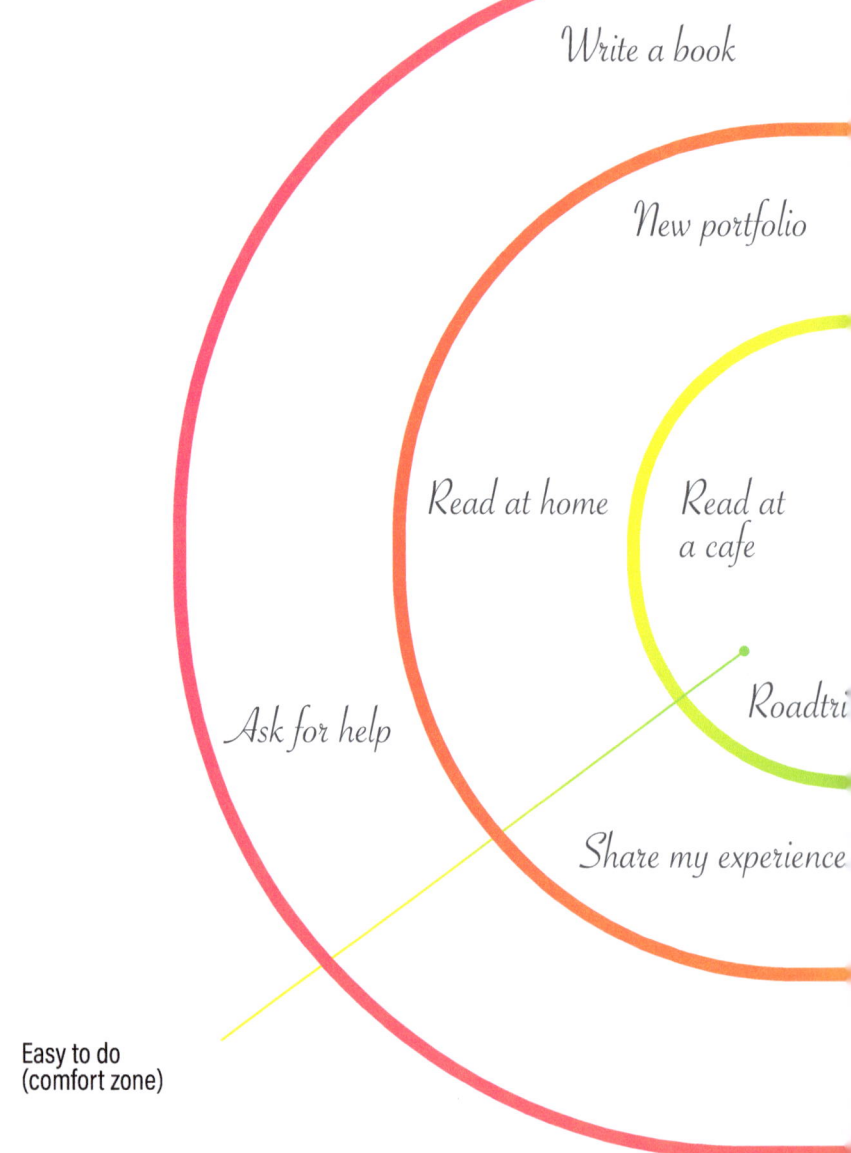

Write a book

New portfolio

Read at home

Read at a cafe

Ask for help

Roadtri

Share my experience

Easy to do
(comfort zone)

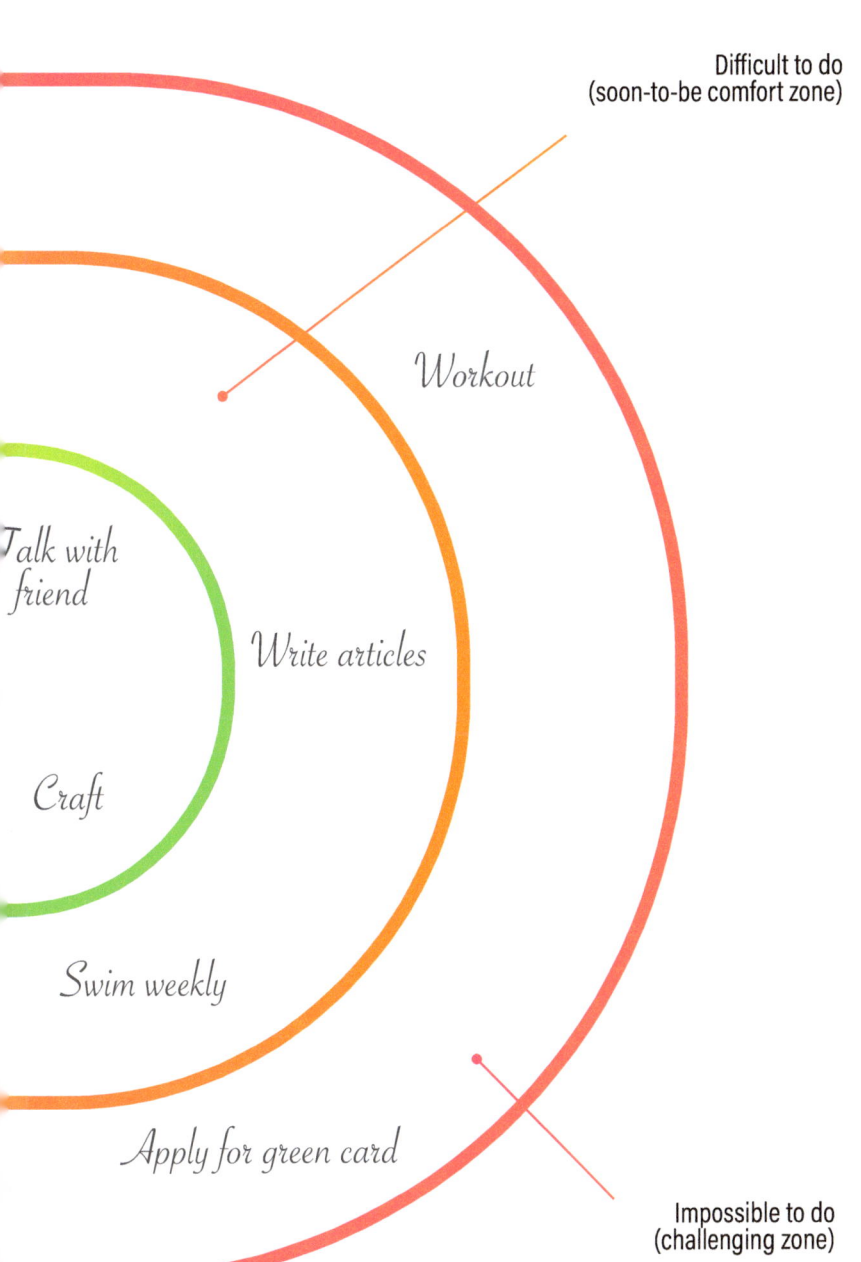

Difficult to do
(soon-to-be comfort zone)

Workout

Talk with friend

Write articles

Craft

Swim weekly

Apply for green card

Impossible to do
(challenging zone)

Let's add our goals in this comfort zone wheel.

Easy to do
(comfort zone)

Difficult to do
(soon-to-be comfort zone)

Impossible to do
(challenging zone)

Belonging

From Lama Rod Owens, I also learned the term trancestor. I realized that I belonged to that trans legacy and had some accountability to move the needle for the next generations of queer and trans folks.

Through Lama Rod's teaching, I welcomed the heartbreak and I sat with sadness. I learned how to give love to the pain to get out of the denial, which is more harmful than the suffering itself. It gave me the tools to break generational trauma.

In the book "Healing Resistance: A Radically Different Response to Harm", Kazu Haga (he/him) shares that we need two hundred and fifty years to shift oppressive systems to end racism. A roadmap exists, with small steps along the way. Even though we won't see the result in our lifetime, we work on a collective dream, doing what we can in our time on earth.

It is scary and hopeful at the same time. This concept unstuck me from the paralysis of not knowing what to do. It removed this overwhelming idea that I had to save the world by myself during my life on earth and focus instead on seeing results for the greater good of the collective.

Interdependence is also surrounding us with our ancestors and working for the benefit of our descendants. It's the opposite of codependency, where we need the approval of others and think we can do it all by ourselves. Interdependence is the healthy spot where we give support to others while receiving some too. We live as a community.

We might not realize it often, but we need others. As human beings, our survival depends on the connection we have with other people. This activity will help us remember who is supporting us.

Envision yourself in an empowering moment. It could be the last time you proudly signed a deal with a client, finished a project on time, or as simple as baking an apple pie from scratch.

Imagine the people who would celebrate the success with you, and those who would not.

You can close your eyes for a few minutes to remember the moment.

What did you notice? How did you feel?

People who I saw **criticizing me** or the ones I usually see as my harsher critics

☐ _____

☐ _____

☐ _____

☐ _____

☐ _____

They aren't equipped to give me skillful and constructive feedback because

_____

_____

_____

_____

People who I saw **celebrating me** or the ones I usually see as my cheerleaders

☐ _____

☐ _____

☐ _____

☐ _____

☐ _____

They are equipped to give me skillful and constructive feedback because

_____

_____

_____

_____

Who will support you? Let's add our celebrating folks in our support system..

What did you notice? How did it make you feel?

What was surprising?

Contact the people you saw as applauding you in your vision and ask them to give you three qualities they see in you.
e.g.: "I am doing this course, and I have to find people who believe in me and ask them which qualities they see in me."

Qualities people see in me

- [ ] _____
- [ ] _____
- [ ] _____
- [ ] _____
- [ ] _____
- [ ] _____
- [ ] _____
- [ ] _____

We live in an interdependent community

What did you notice? How did it make you feel?

_____

_____

_____

_____

_____

_____

What was surprising?

What a journey! Thank you for joining me by going through this book. It's now time to take the assessment again and discover where you might have changed. Continue to revisit some of the tools to continue to grow!

1. Listening to our needs and setting our boundaries

- [ ] I feel pressure to work at a rushed pace

- [ ] I make it a requirement for myself to accomplish all my tasks on my daily work to-do list

- [ ] I go along with a decision an authority made, despite feeling ethical conflict

- [ ] I feel at risk of losing my job if I speak up about some issues

- [ ] I reply to work emails after work or on weekends

- [ ] I feel pressured to work during my weekend if my manager asks me to get something ready by Monday

___ / 6

2. Reimagining who we want to be

☐ I go along with a decision even though I disagreed with it

☐ I regularly imagine the worst-case scenario using "What if..." sentences

☐ I am nervous when I think about next year

☐ I don't feel confident that I can reach my goals

☐ I feel very uncomfortable when someone asks me about my goals

☐ I have a hard time not thinking about the potential failure of my ideas and projects

___ / 6

3. Accessing our inner power

☐ I feel like I don't do enough to prove that my work is good

☐ I work after hours or on weekends to make sure my work will be perfect

☐ I get nervous waiting for feedback from a manager

☐ I hesitate to express an opinion when interacting with people in power

☐ I see some unethical patterns/decisions, but I do not speak up

☐ I sometimes feel confused about my perspective due to the opinions of others

____ / 6

4. Finding our interdependent community

☐ I usually isolate myself when I feel disappointed

☐ I feel incapable of talking to someone when I feel stuck or discouraged

☐ I feel like I have to solve every problem by myself

☐ I feel uncomfortable talking about my challenges with others

☐ I feel like everyone has their life together except me

☐ I rarely know which person or community I can reach out to

____ / 6

Report the results from the previous pages: a number six will be put on the smaller circle at the center, while a number one will be on the larger outside circle. Is it different from the first one you did at the beginning of this book?

BOUNDARIES

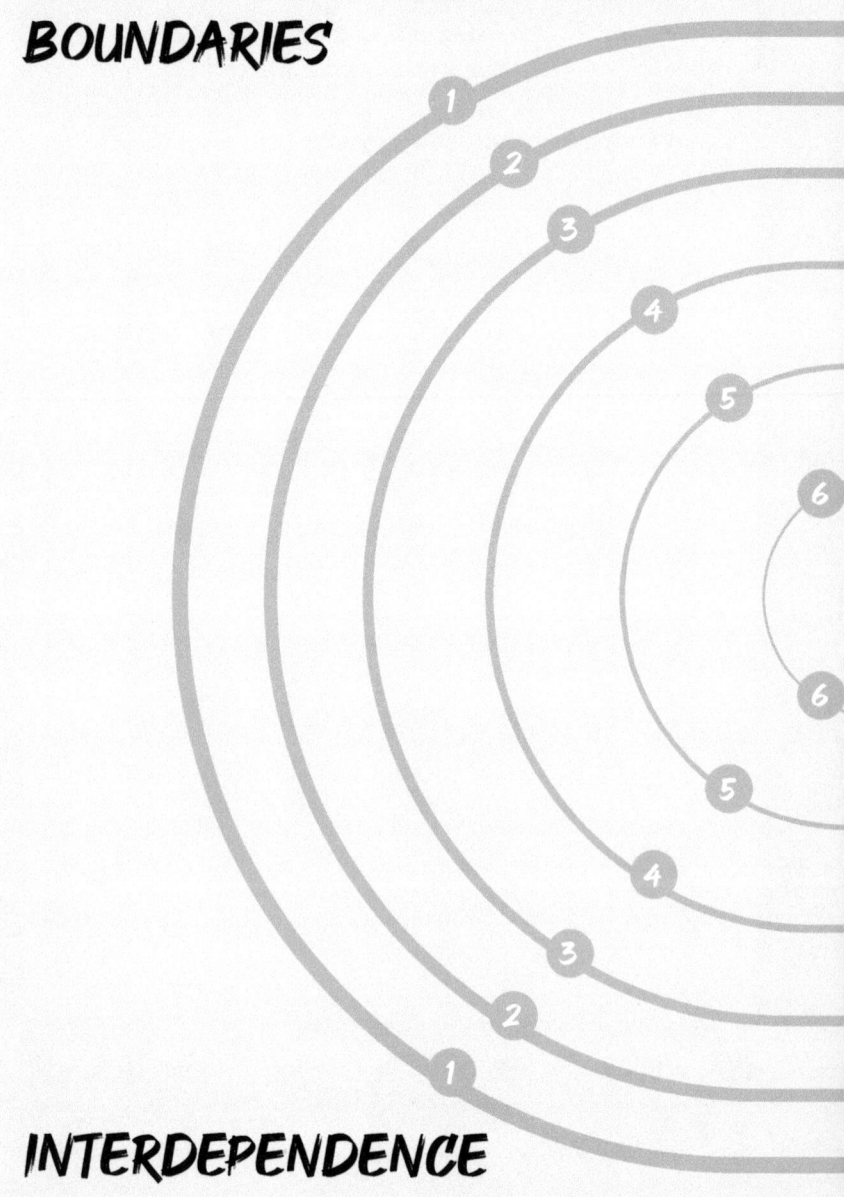

INTERDEPENDENCE

FUTURE SELF

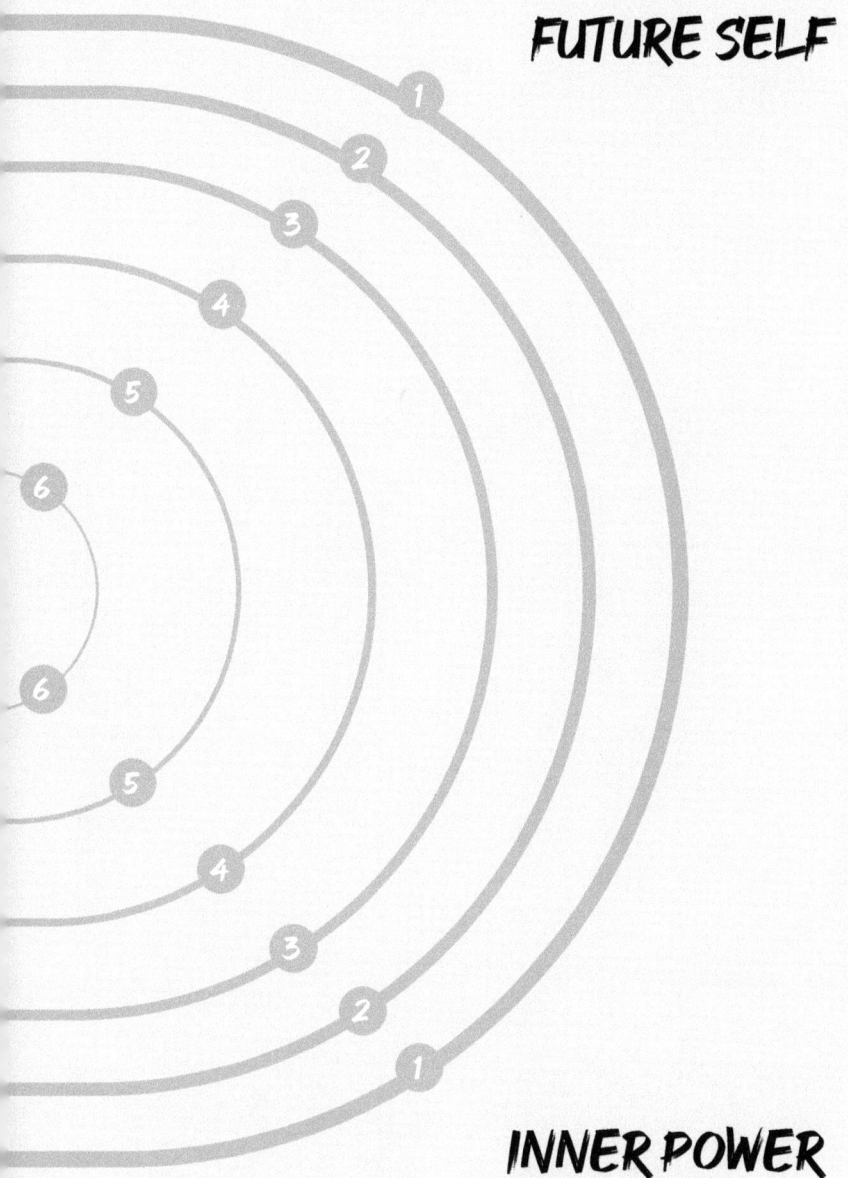

1
2
3
4
5
6
6
5
4
3
2
1

INNER POWER

What did you notice? How did it make you feel?

_____

_____

_____

_____

_____

_____

What was surprising?

OVERCOMING IMPOSTER SYNDROME WORKSHOPS

Take your learning to the next level by joining an online workshop with Max Masure and like-minded folks interested in overcoming imposter syndrome.

"I learned a lot from reflecting on what feels empowering and disempowering for me, and hearing others reflect on that for themselves."

– workshop participant

"I love these exercises as tangible activities I can do when I'm feeling a lot of self-doubt. I already feel better seeing the different kinds of things I'm listing as successes, and how many of them there were. I also feel comforted by sharing this experience with such a warm group of people - Max did a wonderful job creating the space for the trust and warmth that emerged. Uplifting, thought-provoking, warm."

– workshop participant

"It was grounding to hear how it affects others. There's power in having vulnerability shared in a welcoming space. Grounding, touching, empowering."

– workshop participant

YOUDONTSUCK-BOOK.COM

ABOUT THE AUTHOR

Max Masure (they/them) is a community-centered UX Researcher, Diversity, Equity and Inclusion Consultant, Author, and Public Speaker.

Max worked in tech for 15 years, focusing on human-centered and nature-centered design, community-led initiatives, and the liberation of underrepresented communities. Max regularly speaks and hosts workshops about inclusion, imposter syndrome, ethics, and transformative culture.

Max started to live their authentic life as a transmasculine person when they turned 36. Originally from France, they now live in the un-ceded ancestral lands of the Munsee Lenape and Wappinger people, also known as Brooklyn, NY, with their kid and cat.

Photo: Marine Lécroart

HIRE MAX

Photo: Marine Lécroart

Max Masure is available for talks and workshops about imposter syndrome and inclusion. They have consulted and collaborated with the United Nations, Doctors Without Borders, and global corporate leaders, and were named one of the most influential leaders of DEI in 2019 and 2020 by Hive Learning and Engati CX in 2021. They are currently advising the Service Design Network Organization as a founding member of their Diversity, Education, and Inclusion Advisory Board.

max@youdontsuck-book.com - www.youdontsuck-book.com